services. He suggests an innovative program by which private industry can successfully deliver—and often improve—services traditionally provided by government. "Making Our Institutions Work," the fourth section, explains why new approaches must be found to solve the new problems facing business and society, identifies six real problems that confront us, and recommends ways to solve them. In the concluding section—"The Role of Business in Society"—Diebold discusses business's changing relationship with the other elements of society, and he suggests means by which society can be structured so that the most important, most needed services can become the most profitable ones for business to deliver.

The decisions made in the councils of the world's major corporations ultimately have an enormous impact on our daily lives. So whether you are involved in making some of those decisions or are concerned about how they will affect you, THE ROLE OF BUSINESS IN SOCIETY is a book you should read.

A pioneer in automation, **John Diebold** is an internationally recognized leader in the fields of management and technology. The Diebold Group, Inc., the management consulting firm he established in 1954, now has offices in New York, Brussels, Frankfurt, London, Munich, Paris, and Vienna. He holds a B.A. from Swarthmore College, an engineering degree from the U.S. Merchant Marine Academy, and an M.B.A. from the Harvard Business School. Mr. Diebold is, in addition, the author of four previous volumes—the ground-breaking AUTOMATION (1952), BEYOND AUTOMATION (1964), MAN AND THE COMPUTER (1969), and BUSINESS DECISIONS AND TECHNOLOGICAL CHANGE (1970)—as well as the editor of THE WORLD OF THE COMPUTER (1973).

THE ROLE OF BUSINESS IN SOCIETY

THE ROLE
OF BUSINESS
IN SOCIETY

JOHN DIEBOLD

amacom

American Management Associations

Library of Congress Cataloging in Publication Data

Diehold, John, 1926-
    The role of business in society.

    Includes index.
    1. Industry—Social aspects—Addresses, essays,
lectures. I. Title.
HD60.D52   1982   330.12'2   82-71322
ISBN 0-8144-5743-6

First Printing

For Liesa,
who made it all happen

FOREWORD

For many years now it has been my privilege to call John Diebold a friend, and I am proud to consider myself a member of his "inner circle." I am thus particularly pleased that John has invited me to provide a foreword to this book, the most recent in a long line of contributions to the art and science of management stretching back over three decades.

John Diebold is a rare individual, a global citizen who has a deep understanding and appreciation of the values of the old world and who, at the same time, exhibits the vigor, enthusiasm, and foresight of the new. He deservedly enjoys worldwide recognition. His reputation stems not only from his success as a businessman with deep insights into efficiencies and economies. There are many of these. It is also his unique personality which has gained him ready social acceptance among the aspiring, the famous, and the once famous.

Whether by design or otherwise, business has an enormous impact on our daily lives. Thus the role that business chooses to play in society is of the utmost importance, and must accordingly be given the most serious consideration. This is especially true today because of the great changes that have taken place in our society, particularly over the last twenty years. These changes have placed new and different demands on business from government, labor, and environmental and consumer groups. They've presented us with new and different challenges that cannot be met by the traditional solutions and responses. It is therefore essential that business find innovative means of meeting these challenges without sacrificing the free enterprise system in the process.

Exhibiting one of the reasons for his acceptance among the thinkers of the world, John takes a broad-minded, humanistic approach to this subject, which enables him to recognize and identify the causal relationships that exist among the various elements of business and of society. In the same manner as I have seen him proceed in his consulting work, in this book he introduces logical concepts designed to make his readers question their traditional ideas and to recognize that new ideas must be formulated. Once he has made readers receptive, John suggests those innovative approaches he believes will be most effective in meeting the new challenges.

Perhaps most important, John speaks and appeals to a broad range of people in business. For the older generation—those currently in power in our organizations—he offers suggestions for changing things as they now are. At the same time, in his role as a futurist, he speaks to the younger generation—the leaders of tomorrow—with suggestions for how things should be in the future.

Not everyone will agree with all the suggestions John puts forward in this book—I've not always agreed with him myself. But there is no question that what he has to say is of great importance and that his voice is one to which we would all be well advised to listen.

James L. Hayes
Chairman of the Board
American Management Associations

CONTENTS

Chapter 1

FIGHTING THE BATTLE FOR PRIVATE ENTERPRISE

Because business corporations today face a formidable array of new challenges, many people are pessimistic about the future of private enterprise. They forget, though, that business has a long history of successfully adapting to radically changed circumstances. Precisely what are the main challenges facing industry today, and how can those challenges be met? This chapter shows how the business community is pressured by modern political, social, and regulatory demands. It suggests major areas in which business must change in response to these pressures, and it also makes some intriguing predictions about how these changes will shape the business world of the 1990s.

This speech was delivered to the Senior Management Seminar at the Bank of Honolulu in Honolulu, Hawaii, on May 23, 1980.

The outstanding characteristic of the business corporation has been its ability to adapt to new circumstances rapidly and economically. Since its emergence as the dominant form of doing business in the eighteenth century (as the joint stock company), the corporation has flourished in a multitude of cultures and under a multitude of conditions. Within the last century, it has coped with unprecedented changes in technology, basic modifications of wealth distribution and consumption patterns, a redefinition of its relationship with labor and employees, several different war economies, and public and government postures ranging from hostile to supportive.

Today, the business corporation faces an array of external social and political demands that have arisen from changing social values and viewpoints. The increased ability of proponents of these values to publicize, promote, and achieve their goals makes it essential for business to recognize clearly what these new influences and challenges are. Then business can respond.

THE PROBLEMS:
POLITICAL, SOCIAL, AND REGULATORY DEMANDS

That political, social, and regulatory factors have reached a new dimension of influence and cost is beyond question. Their effects are present daily in most aspects of business operations, strongly impacting profitability in many ways. For example, they:

Divert major parts of available investment funds into responding to social needs. For example, almost one-fifth of the total capital investment by the steel industry in 1977 was diverted to environmental concerns, at the same time that the industry, hindered by an increasingly obsolete productive capacity, was laying off thousands of workers.

Delay or stop major plant investments. Hundreds of corporate projects have been seriously delayed or abandoned because of local opposition, based on environmental considerations, to building manufacturing or power plants.

Disrupt production. Federal safety standards are written so stringently that almost any plant can be shut down by the Occupational Safety and Health Administration, creating the strong potential for unexpected disruption. This is compounded by federal agency inspectors unexpectedly appearing at plants—as the Environmental Protection Agency did at Chrysler—and threatening to stop production. Both the interpretations of the regulations and the right of the agency to conduct such inspections are disputed.

Dislocate markets. Recalls of products have become so frequent, as a result of consumer-oriented legislation and demands, that in one recent year, more cars were recalled from the market than were produced. This is not only a matter of decisions made by internal management, but also of government agencies changing their standards and changing interpretations of the law or regulations. For example, one ruling prohibited soft-drink franchisors from setting distributorships by area, a principle their business had been built on.

Require major changes in the mode of dealing with

employees. A doubling of the number of college or university graduates in the workforce has contributed to the growing demands for participation in decisions. This not only changes the style of decision making, but results in new protections for employees and enables them to denounce internal practices publicly.

Place the validity of products in doubt. Government attitudes that accept no product risk have caused significant reductions in new product introductions. In reality, there are always risks, so it is a matter for society to decide how much risk it is willing to accept.

Impose costly and time-consuming efforts to respond to an increasing number of government requirements. New federal regulations are published in *The Federal Register.* In 1970 this publication had around 20,000 pages; by 1981 it had grown to over 60,000 pages! This means that a substantial amount of the corporation's time and energy must be devoted to compliance. In 1978, for example, Exxon had around 1,220 employees who filled out government compliance forms full time. Overall, compliance is estimated to have cost U.S. corporations around $100 billion in 1978 alone. It is plain that corporations must stop dealing with federal regulations on an isolated basis, but rather must organize internally so as to address them on a systematic basis.

SUGGESTED SOLUTIONS:
AREAS FOR MANAGEMENT INNOVATION OR RE-EMPHASIS

The response process for dealing with the new dimension of external pressures will involve several broad areas: leadership from top management, changed internal management tools, and systems of interface with the external environment.

Leadership from Top Management

For any corporation to succeed in the changing sociopolitical environment, leadership must come from the chairman or CEO, no matter how large the organization. There are four aspects of this new leadership role:

Leadership by the personal conviction and example of the top executive officer. This is a very important responsibility that has not been fulfilled, primarily because of time constraints. Time is required to explore the new area from many perspectives; however, time is rarely available at the top level. In order to overcome this, corporations must review their top management organization and, as it were, make time. General Electric, for instance, reorganized by assigning more operative functions to fewer group executives, which freed their chairman to focus on political areas. Other corporations have divided the CEO's role in two, creating a Mr. Inside and a Mr. Outside. The former is responsible for internal affairs, the latter for external matters.

Leadership in preparing the next generation of top management. One of the best legacies a CEO can leave an organization is top managers who are well prepared to assume full leadership functions in 5 to 15 years. Most middle managers have been educated at colleges and universities that emphasized the techniques for optimizing results on the basis of technical, economic, and market factors. Little emphasis was placed on the sorts of external matters that have become so important. This imbalance is further reinforced by the fact that executives are rewarded for short-term results in market or business environments; instead, time should be allotted to initiate them to a broad understanding of the general issues involved. This can be accomplished through formal programs, such as those conducted by the Atlantic Richfield Company; through less formal programs, such as the reading program at Koppers, Inc.; or by simply redesigning career paths to make sure that executives spend time fulfilling the public affairs function (either in Washington, D.C., or within their own companies).

Leadership in balancing the goals of the organization. The organization's system of rewards is usually oriented toward short-term profitability, as reported in quarterly and annual reports, or as measured by reactions to corporate moves in the stock market. The challenge for top management is to complement these goals with an understanding of the long-term requirements of society. It takes courageous leadership from the top executive to forgo short-term profits for broader long-range goals.

Leadership in personal behavior. Increasingly, top executives will live and work in a fishbowl. Since every facet of their personal and public lives will be scrutinized, they must increasingly demonstrate leadership through responsible conduct.

Introduction of Changed Internal Management Tools

The response to the changing sociopolitical environment should be represented by declarations of the CEO and staff, and also by the activities of line managers. Four types of management tools can be used to do this:

Compliance management (with government requirements and with stated corporate philosophy and policy). Traditional profit and loss measurements make no allowance for compliance by line management with thousands of government regulations or with stated—or implied—corporate policy. The result is that top management is sometimes embarrassed and penalized for revelations of noncompliance. In order to uncover hidden problems, new management tools to ensure compliance are being developed. They include incentive systems for managers wherein percentages of annual bonuses are determined by compliance with complex audits and division evaluations. Successful corporations will have to excel in compliance management systems.

Ethical standards management. This is another area not managed under traditional profit and loss standards, though it is necessary if the corporation is to redefine and reaffirm its social values as well as assure its accordance with prevailing public morality. Also, adherence to clearly established values motivates and unites an organization by creating a team spirit. The traditional model for this type of management is the founder or top executive who imprints a broad humanistic viewpoint on the organization (like Irwin Miller at Cummins

Engine, for instance). Some organizations—like Johnson & Johnson—have reactivated a formal set of values to be used to make everyday decisions. Others use a top-down approach in which their chief executive officer explains the ethical code on videotape.

Value management. Corporations need to encourage their employees to develop positive attitudes toward value changes. By helping employees to understand value changes clearly and to see the opportunities these changes present both to the corporation and to the employees, corporations can minimize internal resistance to value changes.

Various approaches have been used to accomplish this. One example is hiring an activist to monitor consumer activities, as was done at Citibank. Another is applying systems of checks and balances, such as the elaborate one of internal consumer ombudsmen introduced by American Express.

Participative management. A major goal is to improve the commonality of interests in existing organizations. Approaches vary from fully participative plans where workers are asking to define the values and organization for a given plant (as in Staley's "old plant" in Decatur, Ill. or I.C.I.'s Locstock plant in England) to community change effort (as implemented in Jamestown, N.Y.) to self-management (as implemented by the Donnelly Mirrors plant in New England). Financially there are also a variety of approaches, like converting workers into shareholders as was done by the Pillsbury Company.

Organization of the Systems of Interface with the External Environment

The successful business organization must organize to deal with or capitalize on new factors. Marketing, labor relations, research and development, advertising, data processing, and stockholder relations are all areas in which new organizational units and management expertise must be applied when needed. Now the corporation must consider how it will interact with at least three new areas:

Interface organizations with leaders of consumer, environmental, and other special-interest groups. Social demands are often introduced in wildly extreme, single-minded forms without any consideration of the costs and benefits involved. When this happens, managers of corporations experience major uncertainties, great demands on their time, and obstacles to planning and decision making in an atmosphere of ideal standards of purity, which no one can achieve but for which they are held liable.

One alternative approach has been to try to establish interaction between the leaders of opposing groups. These informal contacts complement and in some cases eliminate the need to rely on regulatory and court systems. An example of this is the Food Safety Council, established as a nonprofit organization to develop standards for determining the safety of food and food ingredients. The board that governs the council has equal numbers of public and industrial sector trustees. Among them are the presidents of the Public Interest Center, The Nutrition Foundation Inc., and The National Consumers Research Center, along with representatives from such companies as Proctor & Gamble, General Foods, and Quaker Oats. Another example, the National Coal Policy Project (NCPP), brought together leading conservationists and executives from coal mining and other resource-consuming industries. In February 1978, two hundred points of agreement were made public by this group.

Interface organizations with the public affected by corporate decisions. In order to balance social demands with economic requirements, some corporations consult with public groups to try to discover a middle ground that will eliminate extreme positions. Corporations have used this approach to select sites for plants that communities do not want.

Interface organizations with the political system. Corporations today are becoming more and more involved in monitoring public issues, defining corporate positions, forming public action committees, and so on.

HOW THESE CHANGES WILL AFFECT
CORPORATE ORGANIZATION

To respond innovatively, corporations will be required to rethink many important elements of the corporate organization. Six particularly significant areas are the board of directors, the chief executive officer, management goals and incentives, corporate planning efforts, an early-warning system, and a new relationship between the firm and its employees.

The Structure and Procedures of the Board of Directors

The most visible change may come in the board of directors. The board, the focus of much of the critics' concern for corporate governance, will be the target of considerable regulation—whether through a comprehensive corporate chartering or through the evolution of standard practice. Clearly, there is little motivation for the chief executive to push for a stronger and more independent board. One chief executive interviewed by researchers from the Harvard Business School began his comments:

> "I have the greatest board of directors in the United States. The members don't do a damn thing and they don't give me a bit of trouble."

The pressures today are for an independent and top-quality board, one that identifies with the shareholder and the public and not with management interests. Tomorrow's pressures will be even more explicit. Kenneth Andrews from the Harvard University Graduate School of Business Administration suggests that three tasks will be demanded of the board in the future. It will be expected to review in detail management's formulation and implementation of corporate strategy; exercise in a visible way its responsibility to support and evaluate management's performance; and take direct and visible responsibility for the legality, integrity, and ethical quality of the corporation's goals, activities, and responsiveness to society's demands. In other words, there will be pressure for the establishment of specific procedures for the board; liability will no longer be considered sufficient motivation. Indeed, I predict that by 1990, laws, administrative regulations, or commonly accepted practice will demand that:

- The board must have no more than 25 percent inside or former officer directors.
- The board must have no members who are lawyers or investment bankers with a business relationship to the firm.
- Full- or part-time staff must be provided to board members.
- Board members must make a comprehensive public disclosure of their finances, business relationships with the firm, and potential conflicts of interest.
- Board members must serve on no more than three boards, or one if they are executives in major firms themselves.
- The outside members of the board must meet regularly alone with the company's auditors and with the firm's inside and outside legal counsels.
- The board must have two new standing committees not now widespread—a corporate strategy committee to monitor the formulation and implementation of strategy, and a public policy committee to monitor visibly the legality, integrity, and responsiveness of the firm and its involvement in the political process.
- Finally, the board rather than management must handle the shareholder relations function.

The Job of the Chief Executive Officer

There are mounting pressures on the chief executive to spend more time as Mr. Outside, dealing directly with the firm's publics, and to spend more time in Washington, D.C., handling a growing agenda of administrative regulation and legislative inquiry into areas that affect the firm. There is also pressure for the top executive to tighten the reins to prevent corporate scandals and disasters—overseas bribery, chemical disasters, and unsubstantiated advertising. The chief executive's job, already overloaded, promises to get even more so. CEOs must find ways to delegate these new responsibilities as well as tighten the reins without having that effort consume all their time. After all, in the years ahead the importance of the external relationships will only increase. Therefore, the top man or woman will have to be skilled in negotiation, while simultaneously developing a personal credibility that will reflect credibility on the firm. A great part of the chief executive's success will depend on the amount of political power he is able to wield. One projection is that in the future the chief executive will spend progressively less and less time with subordinates, with clients and suppliers, and with peers, while time spent with the board of directors will double and time spent with people outside the organization will triple.

Some firms are already altering the structure of the chief executive's office and job to better handle these new pressures. More and more firms can be expected to do so during the next ten years.

The Design of Management Goals and Incentives

Corporate management already faces considerable pressure for improved social performance in a number of areas: equal employment, occupational safety and health, product safety, disclosure in advertising and lending warranties, and so on. The corporation is under pressure to avoid those missteps that, while seeming to be minor, in effect generate an inordinate amount of bad publicity and do considerable damage to the firm's efforts to build credibility.

In the future the pressures will be for a formal integration of social and environmental goals into overall corporate goals, and for the establishment of management evaluation and incentive systems that measure, reward, and punish performance in social as well as economic dimensions. By 1990 I predict that:

- Firms will have a comprehensive set of social as well as economic goals and will mean it when they say they are of equal importance.
- Firms will have management evaluation and incentive systems that directly reward and penalize performance in social and ethical areas as well as in economic areas.
- Firms will have developed a new set of control procedures to guard against ethical missteps. Such control procedures might include special audit teams conducting what has been termed "process audits" to assess the quality of a work group's procedures.

The Design of Corporate Planning Efforts

How will coming changes alter the corporate planning function? It is obvious that there is already the need for planning to anticipate major shifts in consumer and public lifestyles and values. Firms must do a much more comprehensive job of monitoring social change than they have in the past. The planning function must be able to map out an increasingly complex regulatory and public policy environment, one that all too often suggests unfamiliar demands and opportunities. Regulated industries of the past may have had it good; most large firms will have to understand and manage relationships with up to 50 federal agencies and numerous state and local government bodies. Good corporate planning will take this into account.

By law, administrative regulation, or accepted practice, I predict that by 1990, the corporate planning process will:

- Include an explicit analysis of social value development in the firm's relevant public.
- Permit and encourage formal input from government, shareholders, consumers, and other constituencies, and may be subject to their review.
- Make complex trade-offs between profit/growth goals and the noneconomic goals of society.
- Include an explicit public and political strategy citing how the firm can mold its own public credibility and create genuine business opportunities by participation in the public policy process.

- Be formally reviewed in detail by a committee of the board.

There are a number of examples of corporate innovation in planning that point the way toward 1990. General Electric has conducted extensive value analysis, compiling intensity/convergence charts that suggest issues and demands that are likely to emerge and become a concern for the company. Other companies have developed sophisticated ways of tracking public policy changes, and still others have added people with particular skills to their planning groups—political scientists, sociologists, and even ethicists. Public opinion polls have become standard input for many large firms, and some are designing plans whose explicit intention is to improve their credibility. An increasing number of firms are engaged in regular consultations with unions, government officials, and public interest groups to present drafts of corporate plans in particular areas.

The Creation of an Early-Warning System

The risk of overlooking some social or environmental impact of corporate products or behavior is so high that another new capability will be built into corporations by 1990—that is, an early-warning system that anticipates the impact of products and operations as well as the potential impact of changes in political and social values. Thus, it will be a rare corporation that falls into a major political fund-raising violation, or a major case of overseas bribery—but the challenge here is not to guard against old issues, but to be prepared to face the new ones. Sensitive early-warning systems are needed to alert the firm to potentially threatening value shifts or political moods, and these systems must be able to recommend the appropriate degree of cooperation or resistance that the firm should offer. In general, business has damaged its public reputation by its unilateral opposition to social or special-interest pressures; it must now learn to pick its fights. By 1990, I predict every corporation will have an early-warning system that:

- Includes a public issues group of political experts that tracks public policy developments and analyzes their potential impact on the firm.
- Uses political analysis to help the firm decide when to fight and when to cooperate with new trends.
- Includes extensive procedures for pretesting the social and environmental effects of new products as well as procedures for management to monitor that process.

The Creation of a New Relationship Between the Firm and Its Employees

Demands since the mid-1960s for equality of opportunity and more recently in hiring and promotion are familiar. A scattered pattern of developments makes it clear that the firm is being asked to treat each employee as an individual rather than as part of a group of staff, line, middle management, clerical workers, and so on.

Perhaps in this area more than in others, there will be explicit regulation. By 1990, I believe that the corporation's relationship with its employees will have changed in several important ways:

- There will be no formal retirement age; instead, the firm will be expected to work out with each employee a personal career plan.
- An employee's bill of rights will govern many aspects of the employee-company relationship.
- Conditions in the immediate work group and the structure of work procedures will be administered by a joint management-worker committee.
- Formal procedures and protection will be established for employees who want to blow the whistle on some aspect of corporate behavior that they believe is unethical or dangerous.

CONCLUSION

Each of the changes mentioned would individually revolutionize the business corporation. Taken together, they create a management crisis—or opportunity—of major proportions. The risk of not acting is apparent. If business does not meet the challenge of social pressures, the transition to 1990 will be more difficult and costly. As in the past, the early and thoughtful development of effective management systems to adjust to and deal with ever-changing demands is the only solution.

Chapter 2

WORK IN THE FUTURE

In modern Western society, most people's lives follow a rigid pattern of education, full-time work, and retirement. Rapid advances in technology and improvements in the standard of living are making this pattern obsolete. This chapter describes some of the disadvantages of the present system and discusses how it can be made more flexible to accommodate people's widely differing interests and preferred lifestyles. It presents stimulating ideas about how to reform the educational system, the work environment, and the retirement pension system. The future will bring new attitudes about work, and the business world must be prepared to deal with those attitudes if it is to meet the future successfully.

This speech was delivered to the Harvard Business School Club in Washington, D.C., on March 12, 1980.

The industrial system that made the Western world rich and powerful was described by C. Wright Mills:

> The most alert hours of one's life are sacrificed to the making of money with which to "live". . . . Each day men sell little pieces of themselves in order to buy them back each night and weekend with the coin of "fun."

Our technology, our economy, and our society have undergone enormous changes since the implantation of that system, yet Americans still spend their "most alert hours" making money with which to "live." For some, surely, this is a choice, but for an increasing number of people it represents an intolerable sacrifice.

EXISTING PATTERNS OF WESTERN SOCIETY

The Western industrialized world established—and for the most part has maintained—a strict life cycle or pattern. In it, the first 23 years are spent in full-time education. There is a substantial amount of leisure time, and responsibilities to family and community are minimal. The next 40 or so years are devoted to a full-time job, and often to raising a family. There is very little leisure time, and responsibilities are great and various. The final stage, from retirement on, is characterized by an immense amount of leisure time and few responsibilities. However, because of financial worries (due to inadequate pensions) and the psychological shock of such an abrupt life change, few retirees are able to enjoy their hard-earned "freedom."

Clearly, the inflexibility of this cycle misuses, underutilizes, and cheats not only the individual but society as well. The disadvantages are too numerous to list; suffice it to say that people at every stage suffer the consequences.

Perhaps it might be argued that during the early years of our economic development such a rigid life pattern was desirable. But even if it was then—and I'm not convinced that it was—technological advances and the general quantum leaps in knowledge have now made it unnecessary and undesirable. Indeed, in a world where productive capacity and the technical know-how used in industry are likely to double every 15 years, it would be madness to simply keep raising our standard of living to proportions beyond our real satisfactions.

RESTRUCTURING FOR THE FUTURE

Even in the last few years there has been a major shift in values corresponding to the idea that greater wealth does not always mean more life. The new generation wants and expects fulfillment in different areas—professional life, personal life, and artistic life. As a society, therefore, we are on the verge of a revolutionary change in our lifestyles, and we need to shed old assumptions about what should be done, where, and by whom. Exploring the possibilities of how we might restructure our organizations and our life cycles is the process we must now begin to face.

Education: From Caged Cubs to a Community of All Ages

Today nearly half of young Americans go to college or its specialized training equivalent. The conventional wisdom has always been that in a progressive democratic society, this proportion would continue to rise. However, there are many reasons to suppose that this conventional wisdom is unwise.

For one thing, it is inefficient for society as a whole. If we do all our learning in our first 23 years, then by the time we are in our mid-50s, we will be out of touch with the world around us. If technical knowledge incorporated in industry is doubling every 15 years, 53-year-olds who stopped learning at 23 would know only one-quarter of what they should. In practice, of course, education does continue among top executives, though often in a haphazard fashion through informal study, conferences, and seminars. But in lower and middle management, the tendency to become outdated progresses at a frightening rate. This is one reason why the trend toward early retirement on an inadequate pension is gaining ground.

Moreover, it is not at all certain that, for anything like 70 percent of the population, the later years of youth are the most appropriate for the learning process. In many cases, the years between the ages of, say, 17 and 23 may be better spent gaining experience in other aspects of life. Also, if we do push the college population to 70 percent of this age group, then the remaining 30 percent will come to be regarded as an underclass. Industry already moves away from wanting to employ teenagers full time because any teenagers it gets will be dropouts or those who couldn't even make it to college. An underemployed underclass of disaffected young people poses a very real threat to society at large—and it is, in fact, among these that the high incidence of violent crime has taken root.

It is no solution to say that we must simply step up the equality of higher education opportunity. Of course we must do this. But if we make academic achievement before the age of 23 one of our primary social goals, we simultaneously fix people's chances in life according to what they achieve during the years when they are most dominated by early life experiences. The 10 or 15 percent of those young Americans who come from disadvantaged situations will inevitably go on being disadvantaged. Even scholarships given to such disadvantaged youths are too little too late.

Over 90 percent of university students come from the same age group. Most of them have always known a level of prosperity several times that experienced by their parents' and grandparents' generations of Americans in their youths. They are also better educated and more accustomed to change than their parents. It is only natural that these youths do not agree with their parents about so-called virtues. At a time of huge cultural change like the present, it is important to keep Americans communicating intergenerationally so as to create some sort of compromise about the definition of acceptable behavior. Many older people would get and spread greater happiness if they dropped attitudes that smack of feudalism, racism, pure attachment to the work ethic, worship of the dollar (which was needed to sustain life in their youth but now goes toward the purchase of a second martini before dinner), admiration of existing institutions, and excessive insistence on the privateness of property. Conversely, many young people would get and spread greater happiness if they learned to understand the essential vulgarity and unkindness of shocking people, the evil of physical intimidation, the common sense of certain taboos, and the worth of some of the values that have been inherited from the past. It is overwhelmingly important to create more sense of community between generations, yet we corral more young people for longer periods, keeping them out of contact with the mix of generations that is usual in a workaday business. This separation was especially dramatic in the late 1960s when the huge number of postwar babies born between 1946 and 1953 were moving through their teenage years at a time that coincided with the draft and the Vietnam War.

It seems axiomatic to me that there should be a more even spread of learning, working, and enjoying through the different stages of our lives. This can't be achieved by a sudden and complete reversal of all our existing institutionalized patterns, but there are incremental changes that could help us along the way.

The first general move should be toward more choice between competitive educational institutions. An Englishman, Samuel Brittan, has said of British universities:

> One characteristic of university education is that it is provided at below market prices. Government grants create an excess of demand over supply for places. Thus,

not having to compete for customers, academic institutions are under no market pressures to take into account student preferences. This enables them to run universities to suit their own tastes, whether paternalistic or self-centered.

This inability to vote with his feet—increased by the extreme difficulty of transferring grants from one university to another—makes the student consumer dependent upon a monopoly supplier, a situation guaranteed to create tension and animosity. Although any specific student protest may be misplaced, it is a safe prediction that there will always be some justified grievances arising from the built-in incentives that exist for university administrators and senior staff to suit their own convenience and taste rather than that of the students. This explains many of the arrangements for faculty tenure, the priority given to research and publication over teaching, common pay scales linked to seniority rather than ability, minimal student-staff contacts and priveleged access of senior staff to the more convenient parking spaces, lifts, common rooms, lavatories and so on. Hence, too, the attempts to enforce arbitrary rules of personal conduct or compulsory residence requirements.

Although the choice of universities before American students is much wider, some of the same criticisms are still very much to the point. Universities are likely to be healthier places when they have to compete for students. A condition of government or foundation support for particular universities should be ease of transfer to other educational institutions for students who feel dissatisfied with the education they have been receiving. If universities competed for students in this way, they would also start to compete in providing adults with easier access to undergraduate and advanced programs of study. In general, schedules would have to be made more flexible for students of all ages.

Wherever possible, we should also begin to change the methods of financing universities. We should move from a pattern where the demand for places is automatically subsidized above the supply, to a pattern wherein competition for students will lead to a wider range of students. Other measures might also be considered. For example, business scholarships for retraining employees could be subsidized through the tax system, maybe even wholly subsidized when the student does not return to the corporation but goes into some new form of employment. We could make it easier for older people to enter professional schools. (Many of the country's most able citizens should move from an entrepreneurial to a professional role in their late or middle years.) Student loans could be made repayable in full if the student is below 30 but repayable in lesser proportions for each decade of age thereafter. Finally, private pension schemes could be reformed so that they would, as a fringe benefit, finance a retraining period in college for those who voluntarily forfeited their pension rights by leaving the firm's employ.

Quite possibly, the aim of making educational institutions compete for students is even more important for secondary or earlier schools than it is for universities. Families with school-age children could be offered vouchers equivalent in value to the per-pupil cost of their local school system and acceptable at all participating schools, whether public or private. Poorly managed schools would have to close down when parents bussed their children away from them.

Also underused are the potential opportunities springing from the new educational technology, such as computer-based education, audiovisual techniques, films, television, and cassettes. At present, 20 times more research funding is devoted to health than to education. No major competitive organization would suppose that it could survive if it devoted only a fraction of 1 percent of its operating costs to research and development; yet that is the proportion spent on education today. In large part, the lack of innovation in education results from the fact that it is a producer-oriented industry, not a consumer-oriented one.

If some of the reforms I have suggested were set in motion, I think that we would soon reach the point where there would be many older Americans in college and fewer young ones. The argument in favor of this is not timing alone; an even more compelling reason for encouraging such an inversion might be the unfortunate effect the present monogenerational education system has on American culture—if not the entire modern age. In an age like ours when over 40 percent of American males can be expected to move through higher learning institutions, one would hope for a new golden age of art, literature, music, and scholarship. But too much of what appears seems to be geared to suit the tastes and passions of those who have just emerged from teenagehood. So it may be that changing our learning institutions from single-age ghettoes into all-age communities might create the conditions for a new culture of greater depth and breadth.

Toward a More Rewarding Workday: Flexitime and Job Enrichment

Over the past few years, employers have responded to the growing problem of worker alienation with a number of interesting experiments. Some have been successful and others quite disastrous. Two of the more successful have been flexitime and the small-group system of job enrichment. Both were introduced in Europe, but their success suggests that American business will have to make much greater use of them in the future.

Flexitime was pioneered in Germany. It seems to have been introduced in 1968 by the German aerospace company Messerschmit-Bolkow-Blohm. Under this system, workers can perform their 40 hours a week essentially at times of their own individual choosing. Usually, there are a few "core times" during which it is compulsory for everyone to be present (unless special notice has been given in advance), but for the rest, each worker can determine the times of the day or week or month at which he or she will meet the quota. This idea has spread to a lot of white and blue collar workers at other German firms (Volkswagen, Siemens, Lufthansa), to Switzerland (where 30 percent of the industrial workforce is now on some system of flexitime), and to Scandinavia.

Instead of opting for flexitime, the work week in the

United States has become increasingly compressed. Certain American firms have compressed a 40-hour week into four 10-hour days. Some New York banks and insurance companies have even put computer data processors on three 12½-hour days. Europeans tend to criticize compressions of this sort as unhealthy and unsafe, but it seems that the wisest view is that each case is different and has to be examined on its own merits. In any event, future employers will increasingly have to buy modules of work from the employee—that is, specific tasks to be done at the worker's chosen pace—and if that is the pattern of the future, almost every worker in the United States will move to some variation of flexitime. But within that pattern some people will prefer to work three very busy days a week, while others will prefer to put in five not-so-busy days. Some upwardly mobile people will even take two jobs of three busy days a week, while others will chose one job of one not-so-busy day a week. The successful business will be the one that adapts its offers to buy modules of work in a way that fits its production schedules while making use of these different working arrangements.

The likelihood of this pattern in the future makes the small-group method of job enrichment that has come to be known as the Volvo system especially important. The Swedish naming may be unfair to other pioneers, like the General Foods pet-food plant in Topeka, Kans., as well as a few other U.S. pioneers. But because worker alienation is supposed to be especially high in automobile plants, the Volvo automobile corporation may offer the most useful example. Volvo's innovations include a circular assembly line (so that car bodies can be taken around until they are satisfactory, and there need not be much disturbance if somebody is not in place to put in a particular piece), and a team system of work. The British magazine *Management Today* describes this system:

> Workers will not perform the same job over and over again at a permanent station along the conveyor belt; instead, the 600 employees will be divided into teams of 15 to 25, each team responsible for assembling a complete section of a car—the electrical system, steering and controls, instrumentation, brakes and wheels, and so on. Moreover, the teams will be able to decide for themselves how the work shall be done, including who should do which jobs; and they will be encouraged to rotate the jobs, so that every member will become familiar with each operation in the assembly process. Teams will also have some control even over the pace at which they work, a concession which will be achieved by establishing zones between the work areas to store buffer stocks. These zones will always have to contain at least three units, ready for the next team to handle. But within that circumscription, the work rate can be varied at will; for instance, by alternating sharp bursts with rest periods.

The reasons for this apparent "cossetting of the worker" are that "Volvo needs every year to recruit about one-third of its 36,000 workforce in Sweden just to keep going; and to have about one-seventh of the total force in reserve because of absenteeism." The arithmetic of the decision, to continue quoting *Management Today*, is that:

Volvo is currently pouring money down the drain in training workers who never stay on the payroll; in fact, most of the labor turnover is among people who remain with the company six months or less. The company reckons to spend 125 hours training each new recruit, and is then prepared to devote a like amount of time after the first six months to further development, if the employee warrants it. Using the yardstick of a wage of KR 25 an hour, the full 250 hours will cost the company an estimated KR 6,250 (about $1,350). That figure multiplied by the 12,000-odd employees who in the recent past have had to be replaced in every year gives a grand total of about $16¼ million. Hence even a reduction of a percentage point in turnover saves money.

With these flexitime and Volvo experiments in mind—and with the realization that we too will have almost certainly to break out into newer, more imaginative concepts—the next step is to solve the problem of creating profitable production motivation among workers and assuring them a good life. Before we can do this, we must understand workers' changing attitudes toward their jobs.

Attitudes About Work: Four Emerging Groups of Workers

In an advanced industrial society, it is unlikely that a single attitude toward work would prevail. There are indeed four distinct attitudes, each of which will appeal to different types of people, or perhaps to the same people at different times of their lives.

The imaginatively lazy. Some people—in both blue

and white collar jobs—will not want to work for more than a month or so a year at certain times of their lives because they will be able to make enough money in that month to do something they prefer for the remainder of the year.

The upwardly mobile. More people will at some periods want to work extremely hard in an effort to improve their standard of living. Compared with the 1960s, a substantial number of Americans already seem to be swinging back toward an ethic that recognizes work as one important source of satisfaction.

Those seeking group enjoyment. An increasing incentive for some people will be the sense of enjoyable involvement that comes from working in a friendly group. Employers who want to attract high-quality labor will more and more have to offer this particular satisfaction.

Those seeking interesting work. Forms of work that are interesting to the individual will be increasingly demanded.

Already society has the problem of preventing clashes of interest among people operating under these different impulses and attitudes. In the years ahead, business will have to find imaginative ways to accommodate all four.

THE IMAGINATIVELY LAZY

Within a reasonably short time, an increasing number of Americans are going to be able to earn several thousand dollars a year by working one day a week or two months out of every twelve. Married couples will be able to earn double that, because women's salary rates will eventually equal men's. At various times of their lives many people will prefer very short working years. Some will devote the rest of their time to being with their families or to continuing their education. Others may experiment with starting their own businesses— which may turn out to be more satisfying than remunerative. Still others may use their free time to follow some cultural, political, sporting, or pleasure pursuit.

Certainly, as a society grows better off, its citizens should have more leeway to act as they please. If a man wants to take the day off to go skiing, then as long as he informs his workmates, it should be much easier for him to take a day off than it is now. In the past, this kind of decision has been regarded as slacking—if not sinful— because the absence of one person from a workbench could cause disruption. This attitude will change in the near future. In today's society it is common to say that Bill Jones is a plumber who likes to fish and play golf. In tomorrow's more leisurely society, it may be more appropriate to say that Bill Jones is a man who likes to fish and play golf, and to add almost parenthetically that he earns a living as a plumber. Top managers, whose main interest will probably continue to be their generally satisfying jobs, should not suppose that their own form of enjoyment in work should restrain Bill Jones from doing what he likes to do as soon as our general level of production allows it—which will be sooner than most people think.

The Bill Joneses of this world will be helped enormously by flexitime and by those elements in the Volvo-type experiments that make absenteeism less disruptive.

But their biggest liberation will come when commuting by telecommunication becomes more common than the present physical mode of commutation, and when the normal method of salary payment is not based on attendance but rather on modules of work done.

With modern systems, the cost of telecommunication should no longer vary with distance. The cost put on an existing satellite system by telephoning China will not be much more than the cost of calling the office next door. Computer terminals will speak by telecommunication to other computers all over the world. There will also be a great expansion of telex services and the transmission of documents by telephone. Eventually it will be reasonable for a white collar worker to live in Tahiti and telecommute daily to an office in New York.

The move toward paying white collar and other service industry workers for modules of work instead of for attendance at the office might sound unproductive; but in fact, there will be a dramatic rise in productivity. At present, measuring productivity in the service industries is a very imperfect science. Old methods do not work and new ones are still being tested. But we are now seeing an interest in determining the productivity of white collar work, because of the possibility of replacing some white collar workers with labor-saving machines (of which computers are but one example) and because of the realization that changes in working methods and aims can raise productivity.

I anticipate a gradual productivity revolution in white collar work equivalent to the productivity revolution brought about in factory work two generations ago by assembly line techniques and by mass production. But in sharp contrast to the assembly line revolution, this time there will be the advantage that the physical presence of the worker at the place of work will not be so important and the need for nine-to-five routines will have been reduced. For example, the normal job pattern for stenographers may quite soon be to receive dictation over the phone from one dictating machine in the office to another at home, then to transmit the facsimiles of their work back to the office by wire. The move to salary payments for modules of work done will also create the possibility for making white collar jobs more interestingly entrepreneurial. Corporations that understand the great opportunities inherent in these changes will likely be the most successful.

THE UPWARDLY MOBILE

The energetic, ambitious, self-reliant worker used to be praised as the cornerstone of America. In the late 1960s, it became fashionable to label such a worker as an insensitive, shallow cog. At that time, Charles A. Reich could write in *The Greening of America:* "No person with a strongly developed aesthetic sense, a love of nature, a passion for music, a desire for reflection, or a strongly marked independence could be happy or contented in a factory or white collar job." Now after reaching a low point of regard in the early 1970s, the ambitious, upwardly mobile prototype has returned to favor—but with a difference. Today, ambitious young people want both to move up the ladder of organizational success *and* to pursue satisfying and broadening outside interests. We are moving toward a definition of the complete human being as one who searches for different forms of satisfaction at different stages of life and combines personal goals with goals as part of a larger group—whether it be family, community, or corporation.

The question becomes: What changes can be made that allow achievement-oriented persons to make full use of their talent and drive—both for themselves and for their organizations? Two trends, I think, will work toward their benefit. First, the trend toward payment for modules of work done—rather than for mere attendance—will allow the work-obsessed to moonlight if they so desire. Second, the trend toward allowing work within corporations to be more entrepreneurial for the individual will give the achievement-oriented a greater opportunity to experiment and succeed while maintaining organizational ties.

Any company that allows its achievement-oriented workers to feel dissatisfied will be wasting its most valuable asset. When a firm switches to a Volvo-type group-friendship system, it is important then that individually achievement-oriented workers should always have room to improve and upgrade their responsibilities. One way, already tested in some systems, is to pay people more when they qualify for doing a greater number of jobs in the workplace by passing various tests of ability and knowledge.

The company will also need to establish internal labor exchanges so that workers can choose whether they want to work in group-motivated or individually motivated sections of the company's activities. The workers must have a real choice here. Some will prefer to be retrained at a leisurely pace without competitive pressure, but those who are by nature in a hurry and who thrive on competition and recognition should be given full opportunity.

THOSE SEEKING GROUP ENJOYMENT

Many men and women get their greatest satisfaction through social interaction. The reason many give for why Japan seems to be outstripping the United States and Europe in productivity and becoming the richest area on earth is that its Shintoist-Buddhist ethic emphasizes harmonizing the self with the group. The Christian attitude, on the other hand, is that the ego should be developed within the framework of religious discipline as a unique personal gift. Protestantism emphasizes the individual still more. This Christian-Protestant emphasis on personal accountability to God, justification by works as well as thrift and diligence, was in harmony with the attributes necessary to the accumulation of personal wealth in a free enterprise system. But now that the problem in the rich one-fifth of the world has shifted from accumulation of capital to that of finding ways of getting people to work together happily and innovatively in large organizations, the communal ethic seems to be proving more productive.

American industry cannot convert to any form of Shintoism. But it must begin to concern itself with ways of offering incentives to individuals as well as with finding what makes groups happy and productive.

Middle class people assume that the worst things about factory jobs are monotony and boredom. In fact, a much larger problem may be the bad feelings that often exist between workers and their superiors. Several years ago *The Wall Street Journal* printed some interesting quotations gotten from the convention of the United Auto Workers Union. One young black committeeman from the Ford plant in Mahwah, N.J., said, "They proposed music in the plant and painting things in psychedelic colors, but it's ridiculous. Those things aren't going to brighten up a person's spirits if he's got a foreman riding his back." The head of another local argued that overtime should be voluntary and not arbitrarily imposed. "It's disillusioning to men in line. They'll come up to you at 11 A.M. and say you're going to work ten hours that day. Immediately, at lunch there's a rush to the phones to call home. We're like slaves, prisoners in our own plant."

The most successful of Volvo-type experiments appear to be those that allow workers to run the small groups within which they work. General Foods' experiment at its Topeka, Kans., plant is based on just such a system. Employees are grouped into teams of 6 to 17. Each team selects a foreman and at the beginning of every shift decides how to meet production quotas, assigns jobs, and provides the opportunity to air grievances. Each worker is trained to do virtually every job in the plant. The teams operate semiautonomously, and team leaders have responsibility for hiring replacements and disciplining malingerers. The plant management makes a point of sending shop-floor workers to meetings on local problems and safety rather than sending executives.

One can discuss what it would be like for big corporations to move toward the Japanese system, which tries to keep workers working in the same firm for life by offering fringe benefits such as group holidays, sports facilities, and the like. Plainly, old-style paternalistic firms, which began with single-company towns, are no longer effective now that people have become so mobile. Still, those whose general labor policies encourage workers to remain with them will have a great economic advantage. Companies have to confront the fact that in an age when workers require constant retraining, there is the danger that as soon as they are taught a skill, they can depart to a competitor. Any policy that reduces labor turnover will be extremely profitable.

The role of labor unions will depend on the extent to which they willingly modernize themselves. At present, they are resistant to any form of mobility, including the transfer of manufacturing jobs to the underdeveloped nations of the world. This stubbornness will work against them, as will continuing efforts to impose uniform working conditions on industry—especially when workers are likely to want to choose among different sorts of incentives. On the other hand, the changes I foresee will offer the unions new opportunities. Unions will be able to advise workers and management about which of the group incentive schemes are working. They will be able to bargain about payment for modules of work done. Also, they will be able to help organize increased worker participation—certainly at the fore-man level, less importantly at the board level, and most interestingly at the entrepreneurial executive level.

THOSE SEEKING INTERESTING WORK

As recently as 1940 the average American worker had only an eighth-grade education. At present, about 80 percent of the workforce has gone beyond high school. American society has become increasingly educated, but it has failed to adapt systems of management to take advantage of this change.

Over the next two decades, it is likely that many of the present-day "wage slave" and "salary slave" jobs will become entrepreneurial. This is because the most effective way to secure maximum productivity in an educated society is to make work more individually interesting. The most successful big corporations, there-fore, will be those that transform themselves into feder-ations of entrepreneurs.

There are a number of ways in which corporations can accomplish this. One would be in the way they launch new products, which now is often done in the most unimaginative manner. A firm could, for example, re-lease to its own executives (and maybe even to others) the results of prelaunching studies of products, both those that it has decided to go ahead with and those it is inclined to reject. The firm could then invite bids to run these projects. Sometimes the bids would be made by individuals, sometimes by small groups of friends within the company. Some would be from employees willing to risk their own security by agreeing to work for bare maintenance if the project failed, or they might take a loan from the company to be paid back over the years. Other bids might be from executives who were willing to take the job if they were paid their present salaries, although they would agree to a smaller profit participation later if the product succeeded. The firm itself could then decide which bids it wanted to accept, weighing such factors as its confidence in the bidder, its faith in the projected product, and the attractiveness of the overall proposed terms. This system of assigning projects to entrepreneurial groups within a company would serve to identify the young talent in the company. It would also be an innovative and compassionate way of meeting the problem of senior staff who have gotten into a rut and might otherwise take early retirement.

In addition, big corporations could experiment with entrepreneurial reorganization of many of their existing functions. In all too many large firms there is hardly a department that is the ideal size or pattern. Some departments should be trimmed and others expanded, occasionally by taking work in from other firms on a fee or contract basis. This second possibility could be applied to clerical, packaging, transport, data processing, and production departments. The point is that often things are not done in the most efficient manner, and in the well-run business corporation of the future, reorganization will be achieved by encouraging enterprising members of the staff to submit bids for improving efficiency.

The Later Years: Retirement and Pension Reforms

Only about 30 million Americans—approximately half of all private nonfarm employees—are covered by private pension plans. Under our present system, only about half of those 30 million will ever draw a penny in benefits. This is because pension rights are often forfeited when workers change jobs before retirement or before they have earned a vested pension as a nonforfeitable right.

The result is that America is being divided into two nations in old age: the comfortable and secure, and those who not only are subjected to sudden poverty and uncertainty, but are unable to do anything about it. The division is brutally arbitrary. As an increasing number of jobs become redundant in our expanding economy, it is impossible to accurately forecast who will get the short end of the stick.

For this reason, one might tend to support the idea that the myriad different corporate pension funds should be placed with a limited number of private investment funds that would compete for the individual's pension account. Each employee would own the right to the pension paid for by an employer's contributions and would be able to carry that right along from one job to another. Under some versions of this sort of "money-purchase" scheme, the employee would be able to choose the private pension fund into which the employer would pay.

There are, however, certain difficulties in plans like

this. For one, the reason some private pension schemes look good to those who eventually draw pensions is precisely because they are subsidized by those who have left before retirement and have thus forfeited their right to a pension. It is not usually the employer who benefits when somebody leaves before earning a nonforfeitable right to a pension; it is the pension fund itself, and thus those who stay on to retirement. The effect of allowing the present unlucky half to take their pensions with them would often be to cut sharply into the pensions of the half who stay. This is not generally appreciated by the members of the half who support money purchase systems.

The difficulties are further compounded by the trend toward early retirement, the increased longevity likely to result from expected breakthroughs in medicine, and the continuing growth of inflation and real income. Suppose that we are going to have 5 percent per annum growth in real income in America and a simultaneous 5 percent per annum rate of inflation, meaning that money incomes of those who work increase by 10 percent yearly, or double every seven years. If a woman retires at 60 and lives to be 88, there would be four such doublings (that is, a multiplication of workers' incomes by 16) during the years of her retirement; half of the rise would be due to inflation and half due to the real increases in the income of workers. It follows that if this woman has a private pension of, say, $320 a month on her retirement, then by the year of her death her $320 will be worth only $40 a month in real terms (that is, seven-eighths will have been eroded by inflation) and only $20 a month in terms of her income compared to society's average.

If we are to continue with a system in which people retire at 60 or 65, we will have to agree that all pensions should be increased considerably and regularly after retirement. If we are going to work in an economy where incomes can be up to 16 times higher than they were when granddad was working, then we will have to agree to pay for granddad's pension ourselves (and trust that our grandsons will later pay for ours) because we cannot expect him to live decently on a pension that was created when incomes were only one-sixteenth what they are today. Social security will have to take over more and more of the task of pension provisions, and we will also have to expand other sorts of private pension schemes as much as possible.

The alternative is to work toward a system in which retirement does not have to depend automatically on age. In the ideal society of the future, one might even choose to take, say, four years of one's retirement between the ages of 31 and 35—because of a desire to raise a family or travel around the world. Competitive and portable pension schemes of the money-purchase type should offer alternatives of just this kind, whereby workers can draw part of their eventual pension entitlement early, while remaining covered by life and employment insurance in case they are unable to get a job when they return. The necessary concomitant of such a system, however, is that there has to be no such thing as a compulsory retirement age.

This doesn't mean that there shouldn't be a compulsory retirement age for particular posts—that is for the individual corporation to decide. But men and women in their sixties and seventies should have as much right to work if they want to as anybody else, and they should certainly have as much right as eighteen-year-olds to apply for grants to go to a university, or conduct research, or write plays. It can be said that the worst discrimination in our society is not against blacks or women, but against older people as a consequence of compulsory retirement and insufficient pensions and social security benefits.

SOME RECOMMENDATIONS

What can today's corporation do to meet the problems and changes that confront it? There are, I think, a number of positive steps to be taken. The following recommendations are just a beginning.

1. *Recognize that it is going to be increasingly expensive, frustrating, and unprofitable to operate businesses that depend on people doing work they consider demeaning or unfulfilling.* The sensible alternatives would be either to automate dull and unrewarding jobs as quickly as possible, or move them to countries where unskilled labor would welcome them. It is almost always a mistake to mechanize or automate slowly. Except in a narrow range of craft jobs, as soon as a job can be done by a machine rather than a human being, within a very few years it will be regarded as demeaning for a human being to do that job in competition with the machine. The real problem in this latest stage of the industrial revolution—the automation revolution—is not that we

have mechanized and automated too much, but that we have not moved fast enough.

2. *Start to employ more rather than fewer teenagers.* A good business strategy would include "sandwich courses" whereby high school graduates who come into a business would, after spending some time in paid employment, to be sent to a university by the firm. This procedure could be extended so that it is not only 19- to 23-year-olds who are sent out for sandwich courses, but older workers as well. Eventually, this could become a normal fringe benefit, like a pension, and every worker would be allowed to take off on a sabbatical for three or four years to retrain, recharge batteries, or build a greenhouse. Like a pension scheme, this might be then made portable so that it could be carried from firm to firm.

The corporation should also help the teenage employee become interested in the entrepreneurial or subcontracting part of the business, which ought to be a growing sector of any company. Teenagers in business should not be put into jobs where they "learn" things. This is what they have been doing at school and what they will do later at the university. Rather, they should be given the opportunity to discover which of the different styles of work within the corporation most appeal to them. A teenager who has done that will have a much more sound basis for deciding which course of study to follow.

3. *Take into account the fact that nearly all work will have to become less hierarchically organized, with much less of the boss-subordinate relationship.* Most firms will come to realize that this is in their best economic

interest. Some fascinating research on this subject was done by Professor Rensis Likert of the University of Michigan. His research showed that the "human organization" proved to work most efficiently and productively was that in which certain liberal attitudes prevailed, such as good communications, not too much "yessing" of the boss, and a general feeling of cooperation rather than fear and distrust. This may sound platitudinous, yet Professor Likert and his researchers discovered that when chief executives took steps to try to cut costs or to improve productivity at periods of low profitability, their conventional methods of tightening budgets and cutting waste most often worked to lower productivity and raise costs. It is important that managers come to see their production function in terms of improving the human organization of their firms. This will, of course, require a major change in the attitudes held by management.

4. *Provide employees with much more opportunity for exercising their talents for entrepreneurship.* I have already discussed how this might be done at the top and middle echelons of a company, but it should also be tried at the lower levels. Indeed, in the years ahead it may be possible to maintain efficient production in the more boring jobs only by making them entrepreneurial and thereby exciting. Big corporations should start examining ways in which their stenographer pool, mail room, messenger service, transport and dispatch departments, and so forth can be run as cooperatives headed by the most ambitious people working in them. They should be paid for getting the firm's work done but should be increasingly free to contract to do outside

work (if not indeed contract out the firm's own work) at their initiative.

5. *Measure white collar work by modules of output.* As we move into an advanced industrial society, most of us will be working with our heads rather than our hands, and the great problem in most jobs where we work with our heads is that for a large part of the time we do not know what we are supposed to be doing. It comes as no surprise that even the largest and richest corporations in the world have often not been able to define the modules of output that they require from their white collar workers. And yet maintaining productivity—and profitability—in the future will lie precisely in accomplishing that task. Once definition is achieved, the post-industrial revolution will become a great liberalizing and humanizing and productive force.

Once a business defines the modules of output appropriate to the white collar part of its work, it can give that work to the person or persons who make the most attractive offer. For example, if a firm were about to open a new branch office designed to fill the same role as existing branch offices in other cities, it would certainly be worthwhile to make an analysis of the modules of output performed by existing branches, either by in-house inquiry or by hiring private consultants. Such a study might show that a lot of the work performed by existing white collar staffs is not really directed to bringing forth output at all and is, in fact, quite unnecessary. It might also show that a lot of the real output that is produced by existing branches need not necessarily be produced in any particular place. In that case, staff for the new branch office could often be kept to a minimum by offering existing staff the opportunity to perform some of the necessary work. Then if existing work suffered from this system, the invitation would have to be withdrawn, though even now, there would be many instances where this system would produce far more extra benefits than extra costs. It would also show which branch offices did their jobs most easily, with the most real time to spare, and probably which operated most efficiently.

6. *Apply the small-group approach to labor participation.* The move toward labor participation in management should not take the German form of putting representatives of labor unions on boards of directors (which are then stripped of real power). Rather, it should take the form of allowing small groups of workers to do their own work in their own way at their own pace. Management should also allow these cooperative groups the satisfaction and challenge of functioning as small entrepreneurial subcontractors, letting them bid to perform some job within the corporation they believe they can do more efficiently than it is being done under the current system.

What then is the role of the labor unions? Certainly, workers should all have the right to professional or union representation in negotiations with their employers. But in a fully employed economy, where there is a full market demand for labor, there is no evidence from any country that a strong union movement, committed to militant collective bargaining, increases labor's share in the national income. What militant collective bargaining does, in fact, is push up cost inflation and make governments feel they must dampen demand inflation by running the economy below its capacity for economic growth. In full-employment situations, militant trade union bargaining probably serves to make the real wages of labor lower than what they would have been if that union did not exist. Labor unions also hold down real national income by defending craft union practices drawn up in the 1930s, sometimes in order to protect old ways of making things that it would be more pleasant and more economical to abandon.

Meanwhile, social interdependence has temporarily given a new technological dimension to labor's power. What used to be confrontations between labor and capital are now really confrontations between labor and the public, and this is happening at a time when traditionally unionized jobs have a declining share in the labor force in all the big industrial countries of the world.

The inevitable consequence will be government legislation that will limit both the union's right to strike and its efforts to use monopoly power to impede change. The ideal would be for unions to seize some of the new opportunities before them and change their mode of operation. For example, workers may reasonably expect their union to keep them informed about flexitime in their industry and about schemes for subcontracting particular jobs to workers' cooperatives; to campaign against compulsory retirement; to use its power to pressure corporations to offer workers a choice among various work styles; and to work to obtain portable pension rights, retraining rights, rights to educational sandwich courses, and sabbatical rights.

It would also be an innovative move for labor unions

in declining industries to enter into contracts with private firms to train their people for new jobs. This retraining could be part of the labor-management contract arrived at during negotiations. It would then be important that these workers be able to move into new jobs for which they are trained. This would mean that one union must be allowed to enter another union's area. Ideally, any individual in any job should be able to choose between several alternative unions. This would become possible once the unions recognize that they need no longer base themselves on the old cry that "unity is strength"—where unity means monopoly bargaining power. Instead, they could base their competitive attractiveness on how well they have done for their members in a situation where the law may progressively be tilted against the use of monopoly bargaining power and toward the protection of professional representation of interests.

CONCLUSION

As we move into the future, one of the keys to managerial success will be understanding people and how they behave—their motivations, desires, fears, and objectives. We live at a time when and in a country where men and women are about to move out of the stage where work is something you do in order to avoid being hungry, and becomes something that is done to add some kind of fulfillment to life. It is an advantage that at precisely this moment we are developing technologies that will enable us to build information systems that will in turn make the scientific study of organizational structure much more possible.

Perhaps this study of organizational structure should not rely on experiences of contemporary business organizations, but should glean successful ideas from other kinds of organizations like the Catholic and Protestant churches, the Mandarin system in China, tribal systems in various parts of the world, and even revolutionary movements and crime syndicates. We must reach out every way we can to move away from an age when most people worked in order to buy themselves a little fun and comfort, into a new age when a person's life is more flexible, more fulfilling, and at the same time, valuable to society.

Chapter 3

THE CRITICAL INTERFACE BETWEEN PRIVATE ENTERPRISE AND GOVERNMENT

Government regulation has profoundly affected the climate in which modern business must operate. Complex and sometimes contradictory regulations require large expenditures of time and money and make it increasingly difficult for business to act. Instead of futilely wishing we could return to the past, we can improve this situation by following the innovative program presented here. This chapter emphasizes the importance of rebuilding people's confidence and interest in capitalism itself, and it also describes experiments where private industry has successfully delivered—and often improved—traditionally public services. The opportunity is ripe for business to take the initiative in ways like these and to change many aspects of its relation-

ship with government, but if it loses this opportunity there will be grave consequences for the
future of private enterprise and our democratic
society as a whole.

This speech was delivered at the annual convention of The Institute of Directors in London,
England, on March 20, 1979.

The week following Christmas a woman in New York returned a child's toy she had bought, with the complaint that she herself had been unable to make it work. The salesclerk said: "Madam, that toy was scientifically designed to train your child for the world in which he will live. No matter which way it is put together it will not work!"

We all smile at this story because we share the sense that things don't work anymore, that everything is more complicated and less effective. We're nostalgic for the good old days when problems had solutions.

THE CURRENT ENVIRONMENT

We can find solutions to our current dilemma by examining today's environment and working back to the root causes of our problems.

Observers often have the impression that government is less involved in U.S. business than it is in fact. If you look only at the percentage of U.S. gross national product accounted for by government spending, and thus removed from the market, you could easily draw wrong conclusions about the importance of the government sector. Today 34 percent of the U.S. gross national product is in government expenditures, increased from 29.5 percent in 1962. Though this is not quite the whole story, it is a forbidding prelude!

Regulation

By adopting the course of regulation and applying it, as we have, more according to emotion than to economic consequences, we have tended to take away the initiative from industry, which is the true creator of wealth.

It all started in 1887, when the U.S. Congress began to pass laws requiring federal government regulation of business. The state governments followed. As is always the case when governments get involved, the regulations and the agencies keep on growing. In the past decade they have run rampant. During this decade we have:

- Created one new major federal regulatory *agency* each year.
- Increased from 7 percent to 30 percent the percentage of GNP represented by regulated industries.
- Increased the number of pages of *new* government regulations of business from 10,000 in 1970 to 70,000 in 1977.
- Established 43 pages of regulations for even the *"voluntary* wage and price controls."

The cost of this regulation ran at the rate of approximately $100 billion last year, as estimated by reliable independent research institutions.

Regulatory hamstringing has led our largest retailer—Sears, Roebuck—to file suit against the federal government on grounds that the government's own policies have created some of the exact conditions that regulations require Sears to correct!

Public Reaction Against the Government

For the past decade in the United States, there has been a considerable loss of public confidence in all institutions. U.S. public confidence in business was down to 22 percent in 1978 from 55 percent in 1966. Confidence in big government has also dropped from 41 percent in 1966 to 14 percent in 1978.

"Small is beautiful" is beginning to be applied to big government. Proposition 13 in California and the ground swell of similar legislation have developed throughout our country. At this time, it is even likely that federal spending may be limited by constitutional amendment.

The tide of public opinion is clearly shifting. Whether or not it can be channeled constructively is one of our most important questions.

The Reaction of American Business

For once U.S. business leadership is not standing by, idly waiting to see how the answers develop. In recent years U.S. business leadership has realized that we are in politics whether or not we choose to be. I don't mean, of course, in party politics; that remains as it always has been. Rather, I mean that business is an important component of the "polis" and has a responsibility to help *shape* social attitudes—particularly as they affect the role of government and labor involvement in business—and not merely to *react* to them.

U.S. business has, of course, always maintained a liaison with government and has, on occasion, lobbied vigorously through industry and trade associations. Many large corporations have maintained sizable Washington staffs for some years.

What is new is the vigor, the quality and, above all, the commitment of senior management to the task. Working through groups such as Business Roundtable, the chief executive officers of the largest U.S. firms have committed a substantial portion of their own time and excellent support staff to such activities as personal visits with congressional representatives, testimony before congressional and regulatory committees, and public debate.

Far from conducting public relations activities, in many instances these business leaders have so thoroughly mastered the intricacies of specific pieces of proposed regulation that pertinent congressional committees have turned to *them* as experts to better understand the consequences of the proposed legislation.

The results have been stunning. Important pieces of federal legislation (such as the proposed creation of a major new department of our federal government, a consumer agency) have been defeated as the direct result of first-class analytical work that shows the negative economic impact of the legislation.

This is an altogether new development on the U.S. scene. Legislation directing the federal government to tamper with the market, which a few years ago would have passed, has either been stopped dead in its tracks or has been substantially modified.

But as hopeful as this development is, we have a long way to go. We have neither thought through what it is we want to accomplish, nor organized to utilize the opportunity.

When we decry regulation, we undermine our credibility with the public when we resist deregulation, as the U.S. airlines and trucking industries have done. We also lose credibility when we seek state aid each time and encourage propping up the old rather than supporting the new.

The times are on our side, but I believe that we are not yet pursuing the opportunity with the necessary vigor and forcefulness required to produce long-term change.

The problem, in this country at least, is that there is too much hankering for the past and too little investment of time and resources devoted to the future by addressing the issue of just how much freedom private enterprise is to have.

Social and value system changes mean it isn't going to be the way it was in the past. We shall continue to have new expectations from workers and the public. We must seek new ways to organize and manage. Above all we cannot *seem* to be advocating the past.

One can find limited examples of many of the things business must do if the deadening glacier of government control is to be thawed. Today there is not the understanding on the part of medium and small business of either the current opportunity or the consequences of not pursuing a positive future program and applying all the resources necessary to the task—manpower, institutional, and financial resources.

A PROGRAM OF ACTION

Business can and must do a great deal individually as well as in associations. Let me describe two important things I believe we must do.

Refurbish the Intellectual Basis of Capitalism

In the United States, at least, the arguments put forth in defense of capitalism, market forces, and profits often sound antiquated in their lack of compassion. They understandably turn off the best of the younger generation. These arguments are only too easily turned to equate free markets with the nightmare of nine-year-old children walking to work at four in the morning across the landscape of hell that the Industrial Revolution made of the English Midlands.

At the very least, we need the continuous support of first-class research to refurbish the intellectual basis of capitalism. We are limited here by the number of outstanding, interested, and capable individuals. To the extent they can be identified as students (graduate, postgraduate, and beyond), they should be supported to the fullest by corporate as well as private grants. The limit here is talent. Financial support is essential but it is not onerous. Such institutions as Ralph Harris's Institute of Economic Affairs do admirable work and should be liberally supported.

Privatization Experiments

Giving private industry a chance to deliver some public services is potentially one of the most effective ways of constructively channeling new-found public interest in reduced government expenditure. At the same time, it provides easily understood and compelling examples of the social value of private enterprise.

There are numerous, though all too often isolated, examples in the United States and in Europe of what we would normally think of as public services being delivered on a for-profit basis—usually at considerably less cost and with more of a smile than we associate with public services!

My own foundation, The Diebold Institute for Public Policy Studies, Inc., has tried to gather examples and create more public awareness of the opportunity for widespread application. Here are some cases in point.

• New York City garbage is collected by some 7,800 city employees at varying costs, for example in the borough of Queens, $209 per household per year for twice-a-week curbside service. Just outside the New York City line in the town of Bellerose, Long Island, the cost is $72 per year for a comparable house and neighborhood for three-times-a-week service from the back of the house. The difference is that a contractor makes a profit on the $72 per year, and the city takes a loss on the $209 per year.

• The fire departments of the town of Scottsdale, Ariz., together with some 27 adjacent towns in five counties, are operated by a private company, providing fire protection at about 25 percent of the cost in similar communities. The lower cost is due to a variety of innovations in the use of equipment, which they developed themselves, and, of course, to the fact that they make a profit.

• Dade County in the state of Florida has reduced by one-third the cost of childrens' day-care centers by turning them over to for-profit operators.

- Illegally parked cars in New York City are towed away and fined $65. The Police Department did this as a break-even operation until recently, when it was turned over to a private contractor who keeps $30 on each car and makes a profit on it.
- In Montreal, snow removal is contracted to 47 firms per winter on a bidding system with bids from private contractors for specific blocks of the city (rather like North Sea oil bidding).
- There are several large, for-profit hospital firms that compete directly and effectively with city-run hospitals. Not surprisingly, a by-product of the competition is that the costs of publicly run hospitals in cities where there is competition is lower than in cities where public monopolies are maintained.
- In New York City's Sanitation Department garages, private mechanics were found to be two to five times as productive as department mechanics.
- New York City finds it more efficient to hire banks to prepare its tax receipts than to have city employees do it. The banks in turn account to the city as to who paid what amount, how much money was deposited where, and so on.
- Some U.S. cities and many of our health insurance agencies hire private firms to run computer operations and programming services.

There are similar activities in Germany and in other countries, but so far they are generally only isolated cases rather than the norm.

As I mentioned earlier, fostering such experimentation in the communities in which we operate is one way to build better understanding of private enterprise, as well as to reduce the cost of government and improve the delivery of these services.

Any departure from traditional practice is bound to run into all kinds of problems. It is, therefore, essential to build greenhouses around these experiments, and to create an awareness that they are indeed *experiments* until the problems can be worked out so that they run smoothly.

But just think of the better understanding this would create for the role of markets and profit! Students in the communities in which each of our firms operates could be encouraged to address real, everyday problems rather than being urged to defend seemingly dead doctrines of private enterprise. If each of our firms were to familiarize its community with the ways in which the people of Denmark and Florida, Stuttgart and Arizona are solving similar day-to-day problems, we could soon privatize traditionally public services.

There are, of course, substantial problems to be solved if privatization is to be applied on any scale. To begin with, we must develop measures of output or results if we are to rely upon contracts that embody the profit incentive. Most public enterprises use input or process measures. New York City, for example, has several hundred of what are called productivity measures. They can tell you in detail just how many men and trucks have moved how many tons of garbage. But the real test is, "Are the streets clean?" Or, at the more difficult end of the spectrum, "Is the child educated?" That is what I mean by output measures.

Although we are not yet even doing the research necessary to answer the question "Is the child educated?", that should not keep us from tackling the large number of day-to-day tasks for which it should be possible to devise measures of output.

Probably most difficult of all is to create enough understanding of the role of profit to allow a firm or individual to retain profit made in the delivery of public service. If we do not do this, we obviously will destroy the incentive for long-term improvement in services. However, the very process of fostering these experiments should help in the difficult task of creating an understanding of the role of profit.

The great promise of going about our public tasks in this manner is that if we are successful we shall begin to see the shift from labor-intensive public services to capital-intensive ones. It is insane in our age to allow essential services to remain labor-intensive. Yet that is the reality of all but a few of our public services. Cost inflation can only lead to constant cuts and declining quality.

The benefits of science applied through technology that have done so much for improved productivity in the private sector are virtually unknown in the public sector. While there are occasional programs aimed at applying science to public services, they are very limited. Without the profit motive there is no demand pull, which in other areas ensures a continuous application of science, technology, and, above all, innovation. The profit motive provides that incentive. When it is absent, as it is in the public service, the incentive withers—and productivity withers too. In fact, the incentives in government are almost always against innovation. Even the best managers, when deprived of the feedback of market forces, are unable to function efficiently.

Just as confiscatory taxation can destroy incentive in the private sector and, with it, innovation and productivity, so the lack of institutional incentive in the public sector keeps productivity low and keeps innovation to a minimum. The services remain labor-intensive and, increasingly, prohibitively expensive.

Privatization, for all its difficulties, offers a solution. That is more than I see in the state-run services of the socialist world.

I keep behind my desk the original of a Charles Addams cartoon, showing two caterpillars conversing, while above them a moth emerges from a cocoon and stretches its lovely giant wings. One caterpillar says to the other caterpillar: "You'll never get me up in one of those things."

CONCLUSION

The times are changing for the broad problem of maintaining a healthy private sector. For all the negativism about business, there is a widespread realization that more government is not the answer either.

Refurbishing and keeping up to date the intellectual

basis of capitalism, and fostering experiments to demonstrate how market forces can be used toward politically determined objectives, are only two of a series of things business can and must do if the private sector is to survive. Without it our world will be grim indeed.

Whether business leadership will take the bit in its teeth and apply the necessary resources is far from clear. All that is clear is the opportunity—and the consequences of not seizing it. There should be no confusion over these consequences. Economic democracy and personal freedom will be lost if business, labor, and government are not able to maintain a balance allowing our institutions to work as society changes.

An American economist, Robert Heilbroner, has written, "Surely the claims of rents, interests and profits; the play of the markets; or the right to conduct 'private' enterprise will appear as archaic as the claims of royalty in the face of democratic revolution." He was describing a time not very far ahead.

I do not think such a state is either necessary or inevitable. But a low profile is no longer appropriate for business leadership. We must plunge into the fray to:

- Create an understanding of profits and markets.
- Conduct ourselves in a manner that demonstrates that private enterprise is responsible and compassionate and that our system no longer depends on the iron-rollers of the nineteenth century.
- Make clear that *more,* not less, dependence on the private sector will help make the institutions of our society work.

But I am always mindful of the wise sayings of our American cartoon characters. As Charlie Brown once said, "No problem is so big it can't be run away from."

If we in the States do just that, we must answer not only to our children for an opportunity lost but to another of our cartoon characters, Albert in Pogo, who said, "We have met the enemy and he is us."

Chapter 4

MAKING OUR INSTITUTIONS WORK

Despite the great promise of modern technology, there remains a dismaying gap between what we can achieve and what we do achieve. Our institutions no longer seem to work. Part of the difficulty is that we still rely on outdated, inadequate processes to solve problems, even though the nature of those problems has changed significantly. This chapter identifies six real problems (not just symptoms) that confront modern society and recommends ways to solve them.

This was the Trueman Wood Lecture delivered to The Royal Society of Arts in London, England, on April 17, 1980.

Each age is justly proud of its accomplishments, and so it is with ours. Major strides in science, applied through the arts of technology and modern management, have produced a society in which, for the first time in history, wealth and leisure have not been confined to the very few. They have given us the keys to unlock what should be a truly golden age in man's history. And in some ways it is. For as acute as are today's problems, we must not lose sight of the fact that immense strides have been made in the welfare of all mankind.

Yet while we have unquestionably benefited in innumerable ways from the cornucopia of material wealth and of knowledge that have so characterized these past two centuries, the keys we have forged increasingly seem to be those to Pandora's box rather than to a golden age.

THE NEED FOR A NEW SCHEME OF THINGS

For the better part of this last half-century there has been a widening gap between what is *possible* in the improvement of mankind's condition through using the means we have at our command, and what it is we are actually able to turn into *reality*.

At the end of his beautifully written and all-too-brief book, *From Know-how to Nowhere—The Development of American Technology*, Professor Elting E. Morison of the Massachusetts Institute of Technology well states the problem I wish to address.

There were, of course, temporary injustices, local inequities, episodic horrors, but on the whole the movement was in a favoring direction. Those who had plodded their weary way, in 1880, through the short and simple annals of the poor, came, as time passed, into possession of automobiles, telephones, television sets, air conditioners, credit cards, fringe benefits, oil heat, major medical contracts, electric lights, old age annuities, snowmobiles, and the 40-hour work week. It was all done in the space of 150 years. By any standards, it was astounding.

It shows what can be done when human energy is released and mobilized by the power of an attracting vision, a general scheme. In fact, it probably was the very generality of the scheme that made it fit the times so well. When a bridge, a light bulb, a steel beam, or a telephone wire was understood to serve the progress of human affairs, men were set free to seek out many kinds of intervention. While men had the opportunity by taking thought, working hard, and pursuing every kind of main chance, to improve their own station, they had confirming evidence that they were also increasing the general welfare.

And now it appears that the thing has been overdone. Even before we have sufficiently increased the standard of living of a single person, we are in trouble...

So how to proceed with the construction of a new scheme?

TODAY'S CONDITIONS

It is my thesis that the widening gap between what we can achieve and what we actually do achieve, in terms of the quality of life, exists because substantial change is needed. We must change the processes we use to handle policy problems and how we make policy decisions if these processes are to be made adequate to today's complex and demanding world.

Our political and government institutions were far-sighted innovations in the eighteenth century; they served us well in the nineteenth and have been modified a lot in the twentieth—but the *nature* of our problems, and therefore the nature of their solutions, have changed.

The more reading one does about the history of the Industrial Revolution of the late eighteenth century, the more one is struck with the extraordinary contrast between that age and ours. With a relatively simple technology and the most meager of tools, our forebears took on Herculean tasks—throwing rail networks across unexplored continents; moving half a nation from farms to factories, offices, and cities; changing the work day to seven or eight hours, five days a week, from what had literally exceeded dawn to dusk seven days a week.

In response to these comments on the heroic scale of nineteenth century enterprise, one might respond: "But today we are more concerned with protecting the worker and individual rights; gauging the impact on the environment; protecting the consumer, and otherwise ensuring general welfare before we embark on grand schemes and regulating their conduct."

My response would be that it is precisely in attempting to improve these aspects of our world that society has shown the least ability to apply the knowledge we have. This is not to deny that life today is in many ways vastly better than it was 100 years ago. What I am suggesting is that it is pertinent to ask ourselves why it is not a great deal better, considering the means at our command.

Many of the steps taken with the objective of introducing more democracy into the political process—from the selection of candidates to committee assignments and legislative procedures in Congress—have produced situations that many feel have defeated their objectives by making it virtually impossible—except in the worst crisis—to achieve forward motion. We have not always had this problem. For example, looking back on the world of his Senate days, John F. Kennedy described Senator McGee standing in a virtually deserted Senate chamber, inaudibly mumbling a speech from a few handwritten notes and saying, upon being asked what it was he was talking about, "Oh, nothing at all important." To quote President Kennedy, "Grand Coulee Dam was built!" For better or worse, things don't happen like that anymore.

Another simple anecdote, a more recent one that brings home in human terms the problem today, relates to the building of what was to have been an integrated memorial library and school of public administration named for President Kennedy. It was announced while the public horror at his murder was still fresh, and widespread contributions were subscribed. Yet it took more than 15 years to turn even as modest an undertaking as that into what was, ultimately, only a pale image of one half of the original plan! Not even in the home city and state of one of the most powerful political families in the country was it possible to get agreement among some 14 political districts to an alternative site for a rapid-transit car yard in order to make room near Harvard for the library and school.

Unfortunately one does not have to look long for far more important and dangerous examples of our collective inability to cope with the demands of our age through needed initiatives.

Today, the term *crisis management* is much in vogue. It is often invoked as a description of political leaders and public administrators really coming to grips with emergencies by making use of the trappings of modern management—communications, computers, and all manner of analytical techniques.

Yet, as urgent as is the need for action on today's crisis of inflation, unemployment, urban decay, energy dependence, environmental pollution, and "you name it," we had better recognize that crisis management is self-defeating when it excludes attention to our most urgent and, in a sense, *real* problems. These *real* problems are inherent in the machinery with which society manages itself and the processes by which we cope with the "you name it" crises as they come along.

Of course, inflation, energy, unemployment, and welfare are real and pressing problems that require our best efforts. But what is also needed is to make the institutions in our society capable of dealing with life in the advanced industrial age in which we live. Otherwise, we are going to expend increasing resources coping with a stream of ever more demanding crises. The risk in this situation is not so much that we won't be able to make things work, but that we will have to turn to more authoritarian governments to do so.

Things don't work anymore because brute force solutions to crises are relied upon. Instead, crises must be headed off by changing the processes by which public issues are worked on. It is the processes used to handle problems and to make public decisions that are not adequate to today's complex and demanding world.

Professor Charles E. Lindblom of Yale has stated it succinctly in his important study, *Politics and Markets—The World's Political-Economic Systems:*

> Boldly conceived major new democratic alternatives have not yet been designed. They may never be, even if their design may someday become necessary to the survival of polyarchy.
>
> Yet new forms seem urgently necessary. In the United States, many citizens fear that social problems are running far ahead of government. We are losing control.

Clearly, the boundaries of problems have changed dramatically. Physical demarcations, often based on the speed at which information could travel, have changed from county lines appropriate to travel by horse, to federal boundaries in the age of railroads, to global ones for the era of jets and telecommunications. Yet oddly, our machinery for handling the problems is often keyed to yesterday's smaller political boundary.

Our problems themselves have been transformed: individual issues have given way to extremely complicated and interconnected systems characterized frequently by unexpected secondary and tertiary effects of decisions. (Low mortgage rates of the 1930s, as much as automobiles, led the shift away from cities and the resulting massive new urban problems of the 1960s and 1970s.)

The incentives unconsciously built into our system are often at odds with the results we are trying to achieve. For example, the "don't rock the boat" incentive in all bureaucracies is diametrically opposed to the innovation needed to cope with new problems.

Major changes in our value systems are involved as well, from the desire for instant gratification, to a decline in religious concern, moral fiber, and values, to weak political leadership, to greater democratization in our organizations, to the "me first" generation, to "you name it."

THE REAL PROBLEMS

I have identified what I shall call six *real* problems— real to differentiate what I consider to be systemic or process problems from their substantive immediate manifestation in the form of inflation, energy shortages, unemployment, and so on. Let me cite six examples of what I consider to be the real problems of our age.

Veto Power Can Obstruct Priority Setting

I'll start with what seems to me to be a serious, two-part problem with our political institutions.

In our continuing desire to ensure democracy in all decision processes, we have created literally hundreds of places where we thwart initiative with a veto. In the process we have rarely created what I will call trade-off mechanisms—ways of proceeding despite all the negatives of a particular course of action because it is necessary that some action be taken.

The second part of the problem is more technical and complex: our inability to set national priorities.

Let me begin with the de facto veto powers we have been busily building into our political structure and institutionalizing at virtually every level of it.

Professor Lindblom describes the problem very well in his study *Politics and Markets*:

> In one of the main traditions of democratic thought, government has been conceived of as presiding over constant redistribution of benefits like wealth and power. . . . The emerging peril to the survival of polyarchy is that vetoes are increasingly cast not simply against proposed redistribution but against proposed solutions to collective problems. A veto of a redistribution—say, of new school budgets—is disappointing to some groups. A veto of a solution to a collective problem—say, of an energy policy—may put society on the road to catastrophe.
>
> A failure of policy-making leaves the entire society in peril. One person's loss is now every person's loss.

How do we overcome this problem and still maintain democracy? I don't think we yet know, but I am encouraged in some of my own research to find increasing examples of informal or outside-the-system efforts. For example, business enterprises are starting to work in innovative ways by cooperating with activists in the introduction of food products with chemical additives and in environmental issues.

As tempting as may be a solution of putting more and more power in the hands of a few wise leaders or a benevolent ruler, I believe we must develop other solutions. Professor Morison, speaking of the best interests of the many, put it very simply:

> The only way those best interests can be determined, even in a world where knowledge doubles every 10 years and $e = mc^2$, is by the *many* themselves.

He suggests that in moving toward a solution we take as a model the way in which English common law evolved—growing out of a series of decisions or choices in particular cases. The fundamental idea is to develop a general policy from a particular case (for example, to start with the siting of a single power plant—rather than an overall grand energy scheme—and to go about this with the creation of an ad hoc group).

> ...a sort of committee of public safety fortified by a staff competent in the assemblage of all the varied, requisite information . . . (formulating the case and presenting a set of proposed alternatives for sites, capacities, means of production, etc.).

A word more about the formulating groups. They should

serve as ad hoc committees, called into existence to study a particular situation. They should have the means to obtain all the appropriate evidence that bears on their special problem so that they may proceed to their conclusions in an "unflinchingly rational" way.

Similarly, political invention of the most innovative kind is required for solutions to many of the problems I'm concerned with. It is fundamentally a political problem to devise trade-off mechanisms to balance our many demands with our limited means, mechanisms that allow holding a course with sufficient constancy to ensure results, and that adjust the political time to the economic time.

It would be useful to get some historical perspective on ways in which we have coped with the need for new institutions or at least sizable changes in existing ones. The eighteenth century was a vintage period for the invention of political institutions. Chief among these was the concept of federalism, perhaps the United States' main contribution to political organization in the world. But the strengths of federalism, in preventing the concentration of power, have become a weakness, inefficiently dividing and checking power, sometimes to the point of paralysis. Thomas Jefferson saw our constitution as a "machine of counterpoises"—a practical attempt to create a political institution to solve problems with power. But Jefferson was also an eighteenth-century empiricist. As Gary Wills points out in his book *Inventing America: Jefferson's Declaration of Independence,* Jefferson foresaw change, and wanted even constitutions revised often. Said Jefferson to John Adams, "One of the questions, you know, on which our parties took different sides was on the improvability of the human mind, in science, in ethics, in government." And, continued Jefferson to Adams, "You possess, yourself, too much science not to see how much is still ahead of you, unexplained and unexplored." That we are today experiencing a need to change some of these institutions is far more a measure of their success than of their limitations.

Here are some examples of what I mean by inventing institutions to deal with new or emerging problems.

• The international financial institutions created at the end of World War II may seem obvious in retrospect, but at the time they required considerable hard negotiation followed by an extraordinary ability to sell Congress on the arrangements that had been negotiated—which were not at all of obvious benefit to the United States (e.g., firm commitments without obvious return). We should take a certain amount of encouragement from that not entirely inapplicable precedent when we today face tasks which require putting what is right and what is needed for the future ahead of demands for immediate gratification.

• I suspect that the development of central banking was another example of a way of coping with new needs of the economy for a degree of stability and flexibility in the money system, in contrast with the earlier concept of the sovereign coining money. The creation of the Federal Reserve System in 1914 was an innovative solution.

• An example of postwar institutional innovation was the creation by President Dwight D. Eisenhower of the National Security Council. Many separate executive-branch agencies of the government are responsible for various facets in order to provide one place where the national security interests of our country could be looked at in the broadest sense—from both a short-term and a long-term standpoint. The role it has played has changed with various Presidents and their advisors and is today beginning to be questioned, but the institution has performed the function for which it was intended. (An earlier attempt of the State Department to establish a policy planning staff in order to provide long-term views against which the short-term day-to-day problems could be balanced has, I think, been less effective in the solution of the task for which it was created.)

Although the last two examples are concerned with foreign affairs, I believe nonetheless that they are similar in many ways to some of the problems that I suggest need institutional innovation. My point in citing these examples is both to illustrate what I mean by inventing institutions and to suggest that some systematic study be undertaken of our experiences in the process to see what we can learn that is applicable to the problems I am describing. One of the more hopeful aspects of the problems is that we are starting to see some solid scholarly research in diverse fields that should help to contribute to a theoretical base necessary to effective solutions.

Organizational evolution is another direction in which we can look for solution of some of these problems. A vivid example of what I have in mind is provided by Harvard Professor Alfred D. Chandler's important study, *The Visible Hand—The Managerial Revolution in American Business.*

> This study does more than trace the history of an institution. It describes the beginnings of a new economic function—that of administrative coordination and allocation—and the coming of a new sub-species of economic man—the salaried manager—to carry out this function. Technological innovation, the rapid growth and spread of population, and expending per capita income made the processes of production and distribution more complex and increased the speed and volume of the flow of materials through them. Existing market mechanisms are often no longer able to coordinate these flows effectively.

> The new technologies and expanding markets thus created for the first time a need for administrative coordination. To carry out this function, entrepreneurs built multi-unit business enterprises and hired the managers needed to administer them.

Is there not a public sector counterpart—both in need and opportunity—to what Professor Chandler has described in analyzing the evolution of the modern corporation?

Short Time Horizon

All too often our time horizon is short-term—while solutions to many issues require long-term commitments. As a result, our efforts at solving problems are continually frustrated by the context in which we operate.

We deal too often in the short term, whether in the techniques with which we analyze problems, the terms of political office, or our stock market evaluations of earnings, or financial analyses that emphasize discounted cash flow. In the process we ignore simple and, if timely, low-cost moves that could avert or ameliorate longer-term problems. Short-term decisions may make sense for the individual manager or politician or investor, but they are bad for our society. They lead to high-cost crisis-type solutions.

If problems are tackled in a coherent manner, no magic is necessary to alter our structure of incentives and disincentives in a way that makes a manager, whether of a town or a business, act and think in terms of society's long-term interests. In many cases, it's simply a matter of perceiving the long term as a palpable reality; it depends on political leadership and on the creation of a climate in which we recapture a concern for our children and give credit to decisions that may sacrifice today's gratification to tomorrow's benefit. But learning how to make this kind of change in our decision process is a very real problem.

We could learn a great deal by studying the way in which other societies, including some in different periods of history, have managed to achieve a long-term view in the resolution of problems. The private sector difference between the generally longer-term view taken by German and Japanese firms as opposed to the short-term view taken by many U.S. businesses might be due to the difference in the way each society finances business. In both Germany and Japan, the banks play very different roles than in the United States. There is a dramatically higher debt-to-equity ratio, and much of the equity is held by the banks. In addition to what seems to be longer-term perspective, in many product development and investment decisions I have again and again seen much higher prices paid by both German and Japanese concerns for acquisitions which are important for long-term positioning purposes than is typically considered to be appropriate by U.S. firms. There undoubtedly are other and perhaps far more important forces at work—such as the longer-term employment expectations in the same firm and the realization that one will be living with the results of decisions for a long time.

As with other *real* problems, no easy solutions are at hand. But there are such sizable differences between, for example, the very short-term horizon currently characterizing both public and private U.S. decision making on the one hand, and that in Japan and Germany on the other, that I suspect we could learn much from explicit study of the causes of these differences.

Present Impact of Discernible Future Change

We do not have distant early-warning systems to anticipate future consequences of current and past decisions, to foresee the problems they may pose, and to delineate the trade-offs in priority that we may have to make among the alternatives right now.

Many problems do not lend themselves to forecasting; no mid-1950s projection would have included an overnight quadrupling of oil prices, the social divisiveness of Vietnam, or Watergate. But there is a great deal we could know about the consequences of many current actions that we do not really consider when taking those actions. We are reluctant, on a public level, to get involved in that very act of consideration, otherwise known as planning.

While strong emotions and proper skepticism surround the term *national planning*, we do need some imaginative political inventing to allow us to compare the alternative demands on our limited resources, to assign priorities to those ends, and to create incentives and disincentives so that the play of forces in the marketplace occurs within a framework of politically agreed-upon direction.

Several recent innovations in the United States, including some examples involving the invention of new political institutions, point in a useful direction (though they are far short of what is needed):

• The creation of the Congressional Budget Office. As an arm of the Congress rather than the executive branch of our government, it is charged with evaluating and informing Congress of the consequences of proposed legislative measures as well as conducting numerous analyses of current public policy problems.

• The substantial growth of the professional staff of the General Accounting Office. This office reports to the controller general of the United States, who himself reports to Congress but is appointed by the President for a 15-year term. Here again, evaluations of government operations and of public policy problems by an agency independent of the executive branch of the government allow for more perspective. A similar example would be the gradual development of the analytical staff attached to the Legislative Reference Service.

• The National Academy of Sciences. This organization is regularly called upon by our government to evaluate public policy problems in the scientific and technical areas.

In addition to such efforts, we need to take initiative toward solving some of the thornier issues of the future, as well as of the present. A series of what I shall call *institutes of the future*, managed independently of the government and of one another, would be a start. Plurality and secured independence of such groups are absolutely essential. Contrary opinions and the means of sustaining them independent of current popular political outlook require long-term independent funding of such groups.

Providing distant early-warning systems is indeed a formidable task. And I want to make it clear that I recognize just how dangerous forecasting—let alone analyzing—the future can be. Arthur Clarke's *Profiles of the Future* provides the following examples:

> When gas company securities nose-dived in 1878 because Edison . . . announced he was working on the incandescent lamp, Parliament set up a committee to look into the matter. The distinguished witnesses reported, to the relief of the gas companies, that Edison's ideas were "good

enough for our transatlantic friends, but unworthy of practical or scientific men."

To taken another of his examples:

> When the existence of the 200-mile-range V-2 was disclosed to an astonished world, there was considerable speculation about intercontinental missiles. This was firmly squashed by Dr. Vannevar Bush, the civilian general of the United States war effort, in evidence before a Senate committee on December 3, 1945. Dr. Bush stated: "I say, technically, I don't think anyone in the world knows how to do such a thing, and I feel confident that it will not be done for a very long period of time to come. . . . I think we can leave that out of our thinking. I wish the American public would leave that out of their thinking."

Somewhat earlier, Lord Cherwell had advised the Churchill government that the V-2 itself was only a propaganda rumor!

Some time *after* President Eisenhower had announced the U.S. satellite program, the astronomer royal of Great Britain, when asked his opinion, stated: "Space travel is utter bilge."

Despite many more examples, there is a great deal we can and must learn from exploration of the future, and it should play more than a casual role in our public policy process. In going about this we should take an innovative approach. Fred Pohl, a leader in science fiction, has written:

It isn't really science fiction's business to describe what science is going to find. It is much more science fiction's business to say what the human race will make of it all. In fact, science fiction does better than any other tool available—it gives us a look at the consequences. And it does it superbly.

The views of Arthur Clarke are somewhat similar:

> Only readers or writers of science fiction were really competent to discuss the possibilities of the future. A full consideration of future prospects requires the kind of speculative imagination—together with what Coleridge poetically called "willing suspension of disbelief" which can only be found in the realism of science fiction.

In his *Profiles of the Future* Mr. Clarke gives a wonderful example in support of the role of imagination in any such work:

> Friar Roger Bacon (1214-1292) imagined optical instruments and mechanically propelled boats and flying machines—devices far beyond the existing or even foreseeable technology of his time. It is hard to believe that these words were written in the 13th century: "Instruments may be made by which the largest ships, with only one man guiding them, will be carried with greater velocity than if they were full of sailors. Chariots may be constructed that will move with incredible rapidity without the help of animals. Instruments of flying may be formed in which a man, sitting at his ease and meditating in any subject, may beat the air with his artificial wings after the

manner of birds . . . as also machines which will enable
men to walk at the bottom of the seas. . . ." This passage
is a triumph of imagination over hard fact. Everything in
it has come true, yet at the same time it was written it was
more an act of faith than of logic. It is probable that all
long-range prediction, if it is to be accurate, must be of
this nature.

Delivery of Public Services

No amount of reorganization or management efficiency is going to convert increasingly unproductive,
labor-intensive public services into anything other than
a continuing decline in quality and service in important
areas of life.

It is a paradox that many public services were origi-
nally taken over by the government precisely because
they were so important that we wanted to broaden their
availability and uniformity for all segments of society.
Yet today, it is low-cost, technologically advanced, and
widely available consumer goods—portable color TVs,
computer-driven sewing machines, or cheap pocket cal-
culators with the capability of yesterday's giant computers—that characterize and homogenize society, while
most of the truly important activities—education, public transportation, medical service distribution, running
of cities—are characterized by the fact that they do not
rely on technology and consequently experience upward
spiralling of cost and steady decline in service.

The *real* problem here is not to continue trying to
push technology and modern management through the

system, but to see if we can't find ways to create the kind of demand pull that, in the private sector, leads to innovation and high productivity.

The need for good public services certainly exists. We would all like to feel safer, live in cleaner cities, get to work more pleasantly. But this need has not been allowed to express itself as what the economists call *effective demand.* In contrast to the high-technology products of the marketplace, public services remain labor-intensive, with the built-in certainty of continuous cost escalation that in turn results in cuts in quality and in the range of services a community can offer.

The problem is to learn how to define the end results we want (output as opposed to measures of input) and then create incentives to achieve them. The natural ingenuity of humanity will do the rest.

Isolated examples exist from which we might learn: street cleaning in California, snowplowing in Utica, and ambulance service in Duluth all reflect lower costs and better services in response to competition and the incentive of profit. If such "straws in the wind" mean the creation in the public sector of the kind of demand pull for science and technology that has produced such success in industrial and consumer products, then we may have found the key to a wholly new approach to higher-quality public service. Our *real* problem is making this kind of change in the process.

In advocating a larger rather than a declining role for the private sector in public service delivery, I want to be quite clear as to what it is I am advocating.

We can no more have a society based on a genuinely

free market than democracy can survive without reliance on market forces. Yet we must find ways of focusing major research and development efforts on public sector problems and then fostering innovation in the rise of the knowledge. All the incentives in today's system are opposed to this happening. As Professor Peter Mathias points out in his book *The First Industrial Nation,* innovation always involves a number of people "responding to the demand created by business anxious to adopt a machine to solve a problem or make a fortune."

I believe that the task is now to move forward in understanding the way we can benefit from the market, not backward toward a "free" market system that never really did exist in any advanced industrial society. As Professor Chandler concludes in his seminal study:

> Modern business enterprise took the place of market mechanisms in coordinating the activities of the economy and allocating its resources. In many sectors of the economy, the visible hand of management replaced what Adam Smith referred to as the invisible hand of market forces. The market remained the generator of demand for goods and services, but modern business enterprise took over the functions of coordinating flows of goods through existing processes of production and distribution. As modern business enterprise acquired functions hitherto carried out by the market, it became the most powerful institution in the American economy. . . .

To devise ways we can benefit more from the market, we need not only to understand the problem but to focus our attention on output and develop precise standards and statements of the results we want. A spectrum that ranges from prompt processing of local taxes at one end to less crime at the other presents requirements that can be quite difficult, if not impossible, to measure. Yet since we make resource allocation decisions daily in the public sector, often nearly blindfolded, I can only believe that such an effort would be worthwhile.

Also, there is considerably more value than has yet been either apparent or politically acceptable in looking analytically but innovatively at the modern corporation as an institution that works exceedingly well—given the ground rules society provides and from time to time changes. Indeed, the multinational corporation is one of the few institutions that actually works well and that was an effective agency for technology transfer long before either the term or concept became politically popular.

We certainly have enough examples of institutions that do not work well. Studying ways to use an institution that is effective in both resource allocation and in innovation can only be useful as we struggle toward a workable system.

Professor Lindblom has come to a similar conclusion in his own study:

> If . . . the relative absence of vetoes in the market system and the ease of innovation are desirable in the great market decisions taken by corporations, might they not be desirable features worth expanding in polyarchy? Market-oriented societies have hardly begun to think through the discrepancy and the value placed on initia-

tives and vetoes in the two different areas. There are both fundamental similarities and dissimilarities to be exploited.

The Need for Value Systems Conducive to Innovation

Though attitudes toward work and personal value systems have changed radically, few large organizations have adequately altered their systems of motivating, managing, promoting, and paying people.

Coupled with the alienation from authority and regimentation that characterize current values, the productivity of the U.S. economy is declining. We need large organizations, and it is unfortunate that they turn off the best and most creative young people. Yet the way we handle people in both business and government agencies has not kept up with changes in values. This tends to create unnecessary resistance to change and innovation.

Innovation in adapting job hours and pay to today's realities could go a long way toward unleashing the energies and creativity of many members of society who are turned off by yesterday's organization concepts and practices.

In part, the problem is one of creating a climate conducive to innovation in both public and private institutions. This goes much further than labor negotiation, though I realize it could stop right there if major changes are not made in the trade union outlook that prevails in this country. But increasing the scope for democracy and independent views at the workplace is something that management can do.

To cite just one example of the prize at stake, progress in the whole new field of office automation—a development that will be as important in the future as computers are today—depends almost entirely on overcoming major human and organizational hurdles, which can be cleared only if a climate conducive to innovation is created.

In addition to—and separate from—the problem of climate *within* large organizations is the need to create *external* conditions that favor venture capital, risk taking, and innovation. The vigor and dynamism essential to economic survival require it.

Innovative approaches to manpower used abroad have proven highly successful (notably, the Japanese system of lifetime employment and some of the European experiments involving workers in decision making near the work station). The policies of guaranteeing job security and of involving workers in decision-making processes in Japan and Germany, respectively, are thought in those countries to have contributed significantly to their respective "economic miracles." The key in both cases seems to be the effective identification of the employees' interests with those of the organization. Rather than concentrating on the specific mechanisms used in Germany and Japan (which, being suited to their particular cultures, could not be imitated), we should look at the underlying factors in their success. High productivity in these cases proceeds from a *social* consensus whereby employees see themselves as part of a vital working community (as in Japan), or where they identify with the needs of industry because they themselves have and feel as great an economic stake in productivity and profitability as does management (the case in Germany). We can achieve this—without going back to our 1950s concept of the organization man—by combining the possibility of self-fulfillment with the fact of working within a large organization.

Far beyond what are today the conventional social responsibility issues is the problem of material changes in the way we organize and operate large companies. There is a new dimension to management in the future, from tying management compensation to budgeted non-financial goals, to innovation in the way businesses relate to activist groups, through learning how to integrate sociopolitical and societal value system changes into corporate plans and the motivation of line managers. Much of this has yet to be invented, and whole new subfields of management are coming into existence—from the management of compliance to ethical standards management to devising tools for value management. The political and value system analyses that must be used by managers in the evolution of our institutions to allow a more workable society are still for the most part in the experimental stage.

We Need a Guiding Vision

If we are able to achieve the new forms we need for organization and the new means we need for administration, they can be measured only within the context of the need for a guiding vision. A guiding vision provides what we need most: a definition of our society's objectives. As Professor Morison points out:

The last great scheme for attracting and organizing the energies of men conformed to many of the requirements for good working vision. This was the concept of Progress that dominated the Western world for a century from the defeat of Napoleon at Waterloo to the pistol shot at Sarajevo in 1914.

We need to devise a new understanding of the idea of progress and give highest priority to finding consensus in a guiding vision. Professor Morison ends his treatise with these words:

> Nobody really knows the truth in these matters. We have just begun to think about the situation. But it may be suggested to the thinkers that the problem before us is only partly biological or economic. It is part artistic. One half of art is finding proper structures—whether the sonata form or frame of government—within which the raw data of existence can be processed—made intelligible. Given such a context—neither so vague as anarchy nor as specific as a procrustean bed—the imagination, which abhors the steady set, may proceed, perhaps, indefinitely to novel combinations and interpretations of the data. Indeed the proper frame for its exercise, it may turn out to be the one inexhaustible resource that we have.

CONCLUSION

I would like to suggest the importance that focal points can play in any important change. Looking back again to the experiences of the nineteenth century, we remember the Crystal Palace Exhibit as a striking focal point in helping people realize just how momentous were the developments of the Industrial Revolution. This exhibit signaled the arrival of a new era in British history.

Might we not again do much to focus attention on the problems of making our institutions work in the new age in which we live? From exploring alternatives for a new guiding vision to encouraging the art of social and institutional innovation and experiment, there is so much that needs doing if we are to make our institutions and our society work. Such an effort could go a long way toward closing the gap between what we *can* achieve and what we *do* achieve.

Chapter 5

THE ROLE OF BUSINESS IN SOCIETY

During the next few decades, rapidly accelerating growth in science and technology will bring about an astonishing increase in material affluence. Human happiness will increase as well, provided that our social institutions are able to cope with the vast changes ahead. What will be the role of business in future society? This chapter discusses business's changing relationships with labor, with consumers, with the environment, and with government. Rather than advocating "good corporate citizenship" and expecting business not to pursue a profit, we can structure society so that the most important, most needed services become the most profitable ones for business to deliver.

This speech was a Lakeside Talk at The Bohemian Grove, California, on July 29, 1976.

Competitive enterprise possesses a dynamism and ability to innovate that bureaucracies divorced from markets do not possess. Despite its faults, the profit-seeking enterprise provides the best mechanism we have for spurring efficiency in resource allocation, for encouraging innovation and application of resources in entirely new modes, and for securing the transference of resources to new product lines. Indeed, the dynamics of the market and feedback control through profit—not corporate form or management techniques—make private enterprise the most effective innovator and resource allocator we have ever invented. For society to benefit from this much-needed ability to fulfill human needs, it is the social responsibility of business to pursue profit. The task of government is to establish incentives and constraints in such a way that profit is made doing what society most needs done, in a manner society finds acceptable. Good corporate citizenship is not enough.

In an absolutely ideal world, the social responsibility would be to do just what I've indicated—that is, make a profit. This would be an easy social responsibility, both for capitalist employers and for managers of state enterprises in a socialist system.

In that never-never land, the simple requirement to make a profit would be laid on managers of either capitalist or socialist enterprises as the highest expression of the public good. This is because, under perfectly operating tax and environmental policies, those initiating any activity would have to pay the full social cost of that activity—incorporated in the price of factors of production that they hired (for example, paying for pollution that they caused). On the other side of both the capitalist and socialist balance sheets, the tax-collecting politicians would so perfectly have arranged the distribution of after-tax purchasing power, in both private and communal hands, that business would face the pattern of demand whose fulfillment would bring the maximum happiness to the community. The capitalist or socialist enterprise that made the most profit would therefore, by definition, be the one that provided the most units of happiness at the least social cost; other enterprises, seeing this, would have every incentive to emulate the great and good profit-makers. Adam Smith's invisible hand would be working to the benefit of all mankind.

Unfortunately, in the real world, business people sometimes make more profits not so much by exploiting workers, customers, the community, or posterity, but by deploying resources of time, energy, and knowledge for tasks that society has come to view as trivial when compared to better health, education, and welfare. One sad result of this misallocation is the growing feeling of hopelessness that causes us to forget our great strength: the ability to organize human, natural, and financial resources to achieve increasingly imposing objectives.

FAR-REACHING CHANGES ARE ON THE WAY

The biggest task concerns the future—the task of seizing the almost unbelievable opportunity that science is going to put before us. Let me elaborate.

It seems probable that before the end of the average

lifetime of a child born today, the world will be able to set living standards for all mankind at more or less any level that anybody wants. We have taken about 800 average human lifetimes to progress through 50,000 years of endless hunger and toil to reach the present threshold of comfort and ease. During the next lifetime, during our children's allotted threescore years and ten, mankind will probably step over that threshold. This is not an especially popular statement to make today, chiefly because it is a cheerful one. It is based on two exponential propositions: the familiar one about the growth of the gross national product, and the less familiar one about the growth of knowledge.

The facts about real gross national products are that in the last two decades they have been increasing right across the temperate part of the northern hemisphere—under governments of all political types and qualities—at an average of 4½ to 5 percent a year. If that pace continues, the average child born today would by the age of 80 have seen the gross national product swell 32 times. No sensible rich country today should want to be 32 times richer than it is, and I believe that in practice, the rich one-third of the world will slow its growth. It will, in effect, farm out to the poor two-thirds of the world a lot of income-producing industrial production, in what might be called the multinational corporations' revolution.

The usual objection to this easy arithmetic is that growth on this scale will be impossible because there are only finite resources on this finite planet. To my mind, this ignores the other great exponential factor: scientific knowledge is now increasing at an annual rate of 4 to 5 percent. If this continues, 80 years hence about 97 percent of the knowledge existing in the world then will be absolutely new knowledge. As Norman Macrae, the deputy editor of *The Economist,* has written:

> It will be rather disappointing if within that compass of new knowledge there is not enough to solve the problems of recycling, replacing fossil fuels by nuclear fusion, growing food by means other than the present inefficient method of reliance on unharnessed solar power, finding forms of transport that are less effluent of disgusting exhausts than the motor car (in the same way as motor cars are less effluent of disgusting exhausts than their predecessor in urban transport, the horse), and overcoming the other rather small material inelasticities that some ecologists say are about to destroy all possibility for growing prosperity on planet earth.

In short, we have yet to begin to realize the revolutionary powers that the increase in knowledge will put into our hands and minds.

However, I do not think that the social institutions we have created are geared to move forward at the same pace of advance as is now being achieved in the technosphere. Thus, I think that anyone who plays any part in these social institutions—of which capitalist business is one—needs to recognize that the proper definition of a reasonably responsible behavior pattern is and should be constantly changing.

To me, the really big question is whether the advance to consummate material affluence will be accompanied by an equivalent rise in happiness, culture, social cohesion, kindliness, freedom from pressure and neuroses, and general civility among people; or whether, in mishandling the opportunity for huge productive advance by both capitalist and socialist enterprises, the world may, during our children's lifetimes, crazily cause a diminution of these things. In an article in *Preuves*, Valéry Giscard d'Estaing wrote:

> During the coming decade, economic policy will have to develop at two levels of consciousness. The first remains the strong growth level necessary to meet the enormous human needs not yet satisfied in France, and even less so in the world at large. The second level, which we can only observe in outline so far, but which will progressively come to the forefront of collective consciousness as material aspirations are satisfied, mainly concerns itself with rules of organization and the common goals of a society which no longer has as its main objective increasing its physical output.

New Contracts for Labor

In looking at the future, I'd like to begin with business's changing social responsibility toward labor. In a sense it was with this topic that the outdated political split in most of the present-day world mistakenly began, when it became apparent that the Industrial Revolution of 200 years ago was obliging great armies of workers in the world's richer Northern Hemisphere to move out of villages into factory employment. This meant that factory owners acquired great power over the lives of many thousands of people, and this has always seemed wrong to many of us—including those who have never felt that the best solution was to make the state the monopoly employer. It was on this rock, on this fear that under a capitalist factory system one class would constantly exploit another, that the political split between capitalism and socialism was founded.

As things have turned out, over the past 20 years neither capitalist countries nor socialist countries have ground down the workers to the extent that the other side gloomily predicted. (The doubling of living standards of industrial workers in these past two decades should not be forgotten by critics).

But there are at least two groups of employment problems in which I believe business does now urgently need to pay more heed to its social responsibility. First, there is the problem of those workers who have not caught up. Second, there is the problem of inculcation of the productivity cult; in the last third of the twentieth century we are going to need an understanding of enjoyment culture.

The problem of those who have not caught up largely concerns the two exploited majorities of the world: nonwhites and women. It is a frightening feature of this last third of the postslave century that the dividing line between the affluent and poor in the world is very largely along the lines of skin color. What is happening to women in the rich one-third of the world is less frightening, but often misunderstood. In the last 35 years, there has been an extraordinary equalization of living standards, both up and down, in what is still the world's largest occupation: housewifery. Because of the disappearance of domestic servants in North America and Northwest Europe, and because of the automation of both work and entertainment in the home (plus the birth control pill), there has been a leveling down of the living standards of upper middle class women and a leveling up of others in the poorer levels.

The social responsibility of capitalist business toward the large nonwhite majority of the world and the small female majority of it is to stop discrimination against both. We need to bring much more industrial training to poorer workers in Africa and Asia. Multinational corporations will, I hope, spread the manufacturing revolution there quite quickly.

The huge and unfair gap in today's affluent societies is no longer mainly a matter of money. The gap is that a relatively small part of the community have interesting jobs that are ego-satisfying, while the majority have jobs that are uninteresting and unrewarding.

I believe that private organizations operating for private profit are going to break out of this mini tyranny. And they are going to do so faster than socialist businesses operating under either some kind of workers' control or state control in the name of workers. One reason is that, under both forms of "workers' control," management quickly falls into the hands of a few earnest people who emphasize the need for discipline and efficiency, partly in order to make up for the inefficiencies of being ruled by a committee. Also, a committee of people who think that they are acting in the workers' name will usually be self-righteously tougher on those who offend against the ruling ethic (those who are scabs, or blacklegs, or who simply want to go fishing) than a boss often is on somebody who is not working as hard as he might to earn everybody in the firm (including the boss) more money.

A second reason why I believe private enterprise is going to close the gap between rewarding and unrewarding jobs is that I think modern managers really are at last becoming wiser in the matter of human relations. The Swedish efforts to replace the assembly line with the organization of work in ways more rewarding in human terms are an example. In Germany, they have pioneered—and others have followed—some interesting experiments whereby more and more workers contract to do a certain number of hours work in a week, and within limits they can choose at what times they can do it. This innovation is of potentially major importance over a wide sector.

I am certain that we need to move further along this road of greater flexibility in our working lives, of steadily greater informality in working relations among the educated corps of people who are going to make up the whole of our industrial and postindustrial working force, from unskilled laborer to company president.

This will mean more opportunity for people to choose between jobs where they can work hard if they wish (and get more money), or lower-paid jobs from which they can take longer or even sudden vacations if they want to. It also requires generous unemployment pay and a tax system revised so as to give steadily more specific encouragement to the sort of automation that will most deliberately replace what J. Irwin Miller of the Cummins Engine Company has called "junk jobs—a high school graduate, paid high wages, pushes one red button, or tightens one set of head bolts for eight hours, day after day, year on year."

New Power for Customers

Now to the question of the customers, and of the business and the general community. I think there is something to the argument that in my lifetime we have seen a rather successful people's revolt against being bullied by the big corporations. There have been revolts in favor of the worker, the customers, and the community. And they have coincided with phases when America's top executives have been, in some degree, engineering-oriented, sales-oriented, and now finance-oriented.

In the engineering-oriented phase, under the shadow of Henry Ford, the common people's great fear was that the little man was going to be subordinated to the power of the big machine, and wind up being treated like a little machine himself. Today, the worker is less paced by the machine, and the psychological nature of the situation is greatly altered. My view is that alienation has been more serious in enterprises stuck in old-fashioned methods of production and management—including educational institutions—than in engineering plants.

After the engineer-bosses, business switched to management by the super-salesmen. The great public fear then was that they would create wants rather than satisfy them, and fool us all by their subliminal advertising.

Though they sometimes tried pretty hard, they have fortunately created their own antidote in the form of a more enlightened consumer movement. It is now actually more difficult for manufacturers to get away with such cheating as deliberately planned obsolescence or disguised worthlessness than it was before the age of the super-salesmen began. Moreover, contrary to most forecasts, the cheating is now easier in fields where advertising is unusual, as among doctors or television repairmen, than it is in widely advertised corporate brands.

I would like to see educated consumerism increase, and I want to see an important new technological tool, the consumer data bank, play a big role.

Experience suggests that business has done most to advance the good cause of consumerism on the few occasions when it has reacted most adversely to it. Ralph Nader was largely created (and largely financed) by the huge damages he won when General Motors, one of our biggest corporations, tried to stifle his criticisms by invading his privacy. With the perspective of time I suspect that even most businessmen feel that Nader's victory was good for America, if not for General Motors.

Throughout American history one can make a most unmoral case by saying that our fortunes have been most signally advanced, our people have been served most usefully, when business has behaved most outrageously, and so has brought its own antidote from an indignant public. The bigger dangers have come when business has cooperated as a "good corporate citizen" with government, and especially when it has cultivated its public relations with either politicians or the intelligentsia—because then sometimes monopoly has been allowed.

If the United States had been granted two economic wishes by a good fairy a hundred years ago, the two best wishes would have been that we establish a corporate instead of a small employer system of enterprise, and yet that at the same time we set up a tougher antimonopoly law—that is, a tougher law to enforce competition. Both of these wishes were granted as a result of the actions of, and then reactions to, such blustering, brilliant, brutal, effective, antisocial, and unpopular buccaneers as J. P. Morgan, John D. Rockefeller, and E. H. Harriman.

There were, however, some industries that were recognized early as natural monopolies, or "public utilities," and for over a century there has been a cooperative effort between government and these industries—a federal or local, government or agency regulation of them.

The results have sometimes been disastrous. The object of regulation in a monopolized industry should be to counter a monopoly's tendency to enjoy a quiet life. The specific aims should be (1) to spur the lazy giant forward to meet the technology of the 1990s, and (2) to encourage competition with the monopoly in any way that is economically conceivable. Instead, regulation most often works to try to protect old investments sunk in the technology of the 1920s or even 1890s and to prevent competition.

DEALING WITH THE AGE OF ACCOUNTANTS:
A VARIETY OF APPROACHES

The image of the super-salesmen as great business managers has passed its zenith, and the age of the efficiency-accountants has dawned. We are just now beginning to provide an antidote to their excesses. The main antidote has to be in making sure that the costs they include in their efficiency accounting represent the full social costs of their activities (for example, they must pay for any pollution they cause) and that the benefits for which they strive represent the benefits that the community should demand from the business (so that doctors are paid more when they keep us healthy, not when they give us the most expensive possible treatment after we have become ill).

In the next few years it is going to be right to be fairly extremist in supporting systems of both market creation and tax innovation with these objects in view. I take two examples, both controversial. First, on the environment, I think it is right to move as far as possible toward what is still an unpopular idea: materials use tax. In the version I favor, each commodity would be taxed at its first withdrawal from the environment, which usually means at first sale or import. The rate of this tax would approximately reflect the cost that the item could eventually impose on the community if it is disposed of in the way (of all possible legal alternatives) that caused the *most* pollution. Thus an indestructible plastic container would bear a heavier tax than a paper container, because if you drop it on a dump it lasts longer; and different fuels would bear taxes that would vary according to the mess they exude when burned. There would also be actual payments, out of the proceeds of this tax, to anybody who disposed of these things in a less polluting manner. One of the two big results would be great encouragement for the sale and use of recycled materials (which would bear no tax, because they would not be withdrawn from the environment). A second result would be to make it profitable for wholly new sorts of enterprise to enter the business of clearing up existing messes in competitive ways. The incentives would be to find the dirtiest possible waterway and clean it up, because then money could be drawn from an authority for getting rid of such a lot of effluent; to hire space in smokestacks for my effluent-trapper because I think I could catch more than you do at present and make a profit in consequence; to find the filthiest dump to clear and get money for doing so (as well as then being able to sell the cleared land for development).

Perhaps this system would lead to a few absurdities, but they could be ironed out. The point is that at present we start with the wrong pattern of incentives and then have to make great efforts to get a few environmental controls right. With something like this alternative system, we would start with the right pattern of incentives and then impose a few controls to stop some corporations from making an undue killing out of it.

The second and more general example of a way to deal with the age of accountants is one of the great charges against business: in the rich one-third of the world, private affluence is enjoyed amid public squalor. In some of the rich countries 90 percent of families have television sets and more than 50 percent have cars, yet what should have been achieved in providing housing, urban renewal and redevelopment, crime control, education, conservation, pollution control, the facilities for communal recreation, culture and the arts, community health activities, penal correction, the care of the disadvantaged, and so on—these things have all lagged far behind. A main reason for private affluence amid public squalor is that private enterprise has responded very efficiently in providing those services from which it can make the most profit. Meanwhile, on the other side, some of the services that are rightly regarded as most vital, such as urban housing, have been made unprofitable by government controls.

There are two possible solutions to this situation. I am in favor of what I call the most progressive possible implementation of something that on the surface may sound reactionary, but which I believe to be by far the more liberal of the two possible approaches if we examine the spirit and tradition of liberalism. I think that the market and taxation system should be restructured by government to make the most vital sectors the most profitable areas for every private and public producer to sell goods and services to.

There is a strong body of opinion that would prefer the alternative approach, holding that vital services should not be made crudely profitable, but that industry should no longer seek out only those activities where the biggest profit can be made. As one eminent businessman has put it:

We business managers have hitherto been lucky because measures of our success have depended on one very simple quantitative factor—namely, the measurement of profitability. That's a luxury public institutions don't have. If a college president asks himself, "Am I successful?" that's a very complex question. I think corporate objectives are going to have to be a little fuzzier.

I think that those who accept this reasoning have some awkward questions to ask themselves. Have college presidents, following their "fuzzier objectives," been significantly successful in producing customer satisfaction in recent years? More to the point, have they been able to produce the quality and depth of education which our society has a right to expect? If the efficiency of the whole of our business sector were to be reduced, because of a loss of the profit dynamic, to the recent average level of efficiency of the educational system, might there not be an unacceptable drop in our material standard of living?

Can you operate a mixed system, where inessential goods are produced by factories following the hard objective of higher profit, and essential goods are produced by those following fuzzier objectives? A lot of managers of big businesses would not be at all sorry to see an ethos where they were supposed to follow fuzzy objectives. When you get to the top of a big corporation you have a comfortable life (though you typically go on working as hard as you had to to get there). The only discomfort is that, if you start making losses, people might unseat you, either by bankruptcy, by stockholder dissatisfaction, or by takeover bids. If the capitalist world now says that businessmen should not be toppled when they make losses, because their duty is to pursue fuzzier objectives, then that would enshrine the boards of businesses more comfortably than ever in their seats of power.

It is not hard to understand why people worry about their power. General Motors had an annual sales volume that was larger than the gross national products of all but about 15 of the biggest industrial countries of the free world; it ranked in about the same class as Australia, Sweden, the Netherlands, and Mexico. Few people would question the idea that the peoples of Australia, Sweden, the Netherlands, and Mexico need democratic governments to make sure that their governments' actions are in the interests of all the people. It is therefore rather disturbing that General Motors is ruled by what is nominally a shareholder-elected plutocracy, but is actually a corporately self-perpetuating oligarchy.

On the other hand, I do not think that it is sensible to say that we should elect all the boards of General Motors and every other company—or even part of them. Few of us would turn out to vote, and we wouldn't know anything about the directors we were voting for if we did. The proper course is surely to keep democratic elections for governments generally organized on party systems so that we do know approximately the philosophy we are voting for; then governments arrange spending and taxation and competition policies in such a way that market demand mirrors social demand for happiness, and market costs mirror real social costs. If companies then fail to make a profit under these conditions, they are toppled.

I would believe this even if we were living in a static society. As it is, however, we live in a period when the restless pace of change is throbbing in each of us. In the decades ahead it is probable that we will be able to do such things as artificially increase the intelligence of human beings by injections, artificially change their behavior patterns (for example, making them less violent), electronically stimulate the pleasure centers of the brain so that we can have pleasurable or nonpleasurable emotions to order, set up clonal reproductions of existing people, overcome the great debilitating diseases, put together various sorts of matter molecule by molecule, and so on. Whether we are to allow any of these things should be decided by democratic governments after open, thoughtful, and educated debate, not by business corporations following "fuzzy" objectives.

Explaining why the workers in the immigrant-founded society of America never seriously flirted with socialism, but stayed loyal to free enterprise, John K. Jessup wrote:

> Why did Americans never declare war on the bitch goddess? Why have they mostly supported the capitalist system? Not because they looked to it for social justice. Except for economic justice quite narrowly defined, they looked elsewhere for that. And not because they did not value social justice. They liked capitalism because . . . for people who wanted above all to decide for themselves the terms on which they made their living, a contract society with all its risks and rigors had obvious advantages over

the status societies they or their fathers had left. Capitalism has always offered a greater variety of careers.

My guess is that mankind as a whole in the next few decades will be leaving behind forever societies where status is based on inherited class or wealth, and that the advantage of contract-based capitalism just described may become an important guarantor of freedom. I think it will be important that people from now on can, if they want to, choose to work for a few months a year, probably draw enough wages from that to live at what one would call today a decent bourgeois standard, and then live as they wish for the other months of the year.

I feel just a bit nervous about the new tendency of business to "get religion" and try to act for society's benefit instead of seeking profit. This new concept of "good corporate citizenship" does, after all, involve individual business people deciding on their own what is good for society, and then going out to spend other people's (stockholders') money and other people's (employees') time on it. As Henry Ford II said:

> The corporation is not an all-purpose mechanism. It is a specialized tool designed primarily to serve the economic needs of society—the needs for goods and services and jobs. If corporations devote their attention primarily to other social needs, society's economic needs will be served less effectively.

One of the best warnings about all this is as old as the science of economics itself. In the passage that began with the most famous phrase of his *The Wealth of*

Nations in 1776, Adam Smith wrote about the merchant who is following his self-interest and trying to maximize profit. The merchant thereby actually produces the greatest possible good for society, although he "neither intends to promote the public interest, nor knows how much he is promoting it." Smith went on:

> By directing that industry in such a manner as its produce may be of the greatest value, he intends only his own gain, and he is in this, as in many other cases, led by an invisible hand to promote an end which was not part of his intention. Nor is it always the worse for the society that it was not part of it. By pursuing his own interest he frequently promotes that of the society more effectually than when he really intends to promote it. I have never known much good done by those who affected to trade for the public good. It is an affectation, indeed, not very common among merchants, and very few words need be employed in dissuading him from it.

SUGGESTIONS FOR ACTION: A SUMMARY

I suggest that all governments should assign permanent responsibility to an organizational unit that asks itself all the time: "How can we create new market mechanisms that will bring in a competitive dynamic to try to help meet problems that are not being met today?" I believe that over a whole range of public services we should be willing to move to a technique of competitive franchising. To accomplish this, we should define what the public services concerned are supposed to be doing, set down the cost incurred at present, and then be willing to pay the cost as a fee to any private tenderer who believes that he or she would be able to achieve better result performance.

I suggest that public employers, private employers, and labor unions should get together to draft alternative sorts of work contracts, including work contracts for people who do not want to engage in the normal work week. A lot of employers would say that their own businesses must for a long time employ only people who work the normal fixed-hours-plus-overtime sort of contract, but I think that those who say that all their work must forever be done only by those who do not opt for new contracts will find themselves having to pay more money.

I suggest that government subsidies are needed for the establishment of computerized consumer data banks, and competing consumer organizations with membership or fee-paying revenue sources should be able to use them either without payment or for an annual fee.

I suggest that we need more forecasting institutes: not ones that pledge their vanity on saying that certain events (eco-doom or whatever) are most probable, but institutes that set out possible alternative scenarios and then continually check what course we seem to actually be following. Our present system of forecasting by bouts of hysteria has nothing to recommend it. These new forecasting institutions should be divorced from government so that positions can be advocated contrary to the government policy of the day. They should, as well, be pluralistic, so that diversity of opinion would be encouraged. Relying on a single institution in each field runs the risk of monolithic positions. Intellectual freedom and imagination are of utmost importance in areas necessarily as speculative and as important in today's world as forecasting. Much is to be said, therefore, in private foundations as well as public funding, for long-term financial commitments so that unpopular positions can be explored and presented without reprisals or suppression.

In closing, I quote Valéry Giscard d'Estaing:

> Should happiness lie in the possibility for the human mind to free itself from extreme material constraints and dedicate itself to an effort of culture and civilization, then I am convinced that the road we still have to cover in pursuit of economic growth is indeed one that takes us there, until we discover greatly expanded new horizons.

INDEX